South Lake Tahoe Climbing

SUPERTOPOS

South Lake Tahoe Climbing

SUPERTOPOS

Chris McNamara

Published by
SuperTopo
2 Bradford Way
Mill Valley, CA 94941
www.supertopo.com

Topos and text by Chris McNamara
Managing Editor and Designer: Sarah Felchlin
Editor/Head of Shipping: Steve McNamara
Contributing Designer: David Safanda
Publisher: Chris McNamara

Front cover: Sabina Allemann gracefully climbs on Spacewalk (5.11c), Eagle Lake Buttress.
 Photo by Corey Rich.
Frontispiece: Alexis Calcaño experiences Nirvana. *Photo by Jim Thornburg.*
Back cover: Alexis Calcaño on the best 5.10a at The Leap, Hospital Corner.
 Photo by Jim Thornburg.

McNamara, Chris
South Lake Tahoe Climbing: SuperTopos

ISBN 0-9672391-7-6

Contents

Acknowledgements   7

Preface   11

Introduction   13
  Path to Multi-Pitch Climbing   18
  Crag Comparison   19
  Free Climbing Ratings   20
  Cam Sizes by Brand   21
  Understanding the Maps   22
  Tahoe Overview Map   23

Sugarloaf   25
  Sugarbun   28
  Midway Rock   30
  Dental Wall   31
  South Face   33
  East Face   34
  West Face   40
  West Buttress   44

Phantom Spires   46
  Lizard Head   50
  Lost John   52
  Upper Spire   54
  Shark's Tooth   61
  Clam Rock   61
  Middle Spire   62
  The Blocks   66
  Twin Owls   68
  Gorilla Rock   69
  Lower Spire   70
  Phantom Wall, Right   72

Wrights Lake   74
  Main Wall   76
  Spectrum Tower   78
  Black Beauty Wall   79

Lover's Leap   81
  East Wall   88
  Central Wall   96
  Main Wall and West Wall   101
  Dear John Buttress   108
  Lower Buttress   112
  Hogwild   118
  Hogsback   123
  The Box   126
  Campground Boulders   128

Echo Lakes   133
  Gangsta Wall   134
  Old Peculiar   138
  Berkeley Camp   140

Luther Rock   142
  Distillery Wall   143
  Detox Wall   144

Luther Spires   146

Eagle Creek Canyon   150
  Eagle Lake Cliff   152
  Eagle Creek Cliff   159
  Eagle's Nest   162
  Mayhem Cove   164
  90-Foot Wall   168

Appendix
  Climbs by Rating   172
  Climbs by Name   178

Warning!

Climbing is an inherently dangerous sport in which severe injuries or death may occur. Relying on the information in this book may increase the danger.

When climbing you can only rely on your skill, training, experience, and conditioning. **If you have any doubts as to your ability to safely climb any route in this guide, do not try it.**

This book is neither a professional climbing instructor nor a substitute for one. **It is not an instructional book. Do not use it as one.** It contains information that is nothing more than a compilation of opinions about climbing in South Lake Tahoe. **These opinions are neither facts nor promises.** Treat the information as opinions and nothing more. Do not substitute these opinions for your own common sense and experience.

Assumption of Risk

There may be errors in this book resulting from the mistakes of the authors and/or the people with whom they consulted. The information was gathered from a variety of sources, which may not have been independently verified. Those who provided the information may have made mistakes in their descriptions. The authors may have made mistakes in their conveyance of the information in this book. **The authors cannot, therefore, guarantee the correctness of any of the information contained in this book.** The topographical maps, photo-diagrams, difficulty ratings, protection ratings, approach and/or descent information, suggestions about equipment, and other matters may be incorrect or misleading. Fixed protection may be absent, unreliable, or misplaced. **You must keep in mind that the information in this book may be erroneous, so use your own judgement when choosing, approaching, climbing, or descending from a route described in this book.**

DO NOT USE THIS BOOK UNLESS YOU [AND YOUR ESTATE] PROMISE NEVER TO TRY TO SUE US IF YOU GET HURT OR KILLED.

Disclaimer of Warranties

THE AUTHORS AND PUBLISHER WARN THAT THIS BOOK CONTAINS ONLY THE AUTHORS' OPINIONS ON THE SUBJECTS DISCUSSED. THEY MAKE NO OTHER WARRANTIES, EXPRESSED OR IMPLIED, OF MERCHANTABILITY, FITNESS FOR PURPOSE, OR OTHERWISE, AND IN ANY EVENT, THEIR LIABILITY FOR BREACH OF ANY WARRANTY OR CONTRACT WITH RESPECT TO THE CONTENT OF THIS BOOK IS LIMITED TO THE PURCHASE PRICE OF THE BOOK. THEY FURTHER LIMIT TO SUCH PURCHASE PRICE THEIR LIABILITY ON ACCOUNT OF ANY KIND OF NEGLIGENT BEHAVIOR WHATSOEVER ON THEIR PART WITH RESPECT TO THE CONTENTS OF THIS BOOK.

Acknowledgements

A guidebook is far from a solo effort. To be successful it must be a community project that involves the good work of first ascentionists, locals, and individual climbers who have valuable feedback. This book is no exception, and here are my main sources of information and guidance:

Todd Offenbacher showed me many of the classic areas, new route potential and, most importantly, he kept me laughing the whole time. Todd embodies the spirit that climbing should be first and foremost about having fun with your friends.

Petch Pietrolungo is the owner of Lover's Leap Guides and a living guidebook of Lover's Leap. He put up many of the modern classics and gave me extensive tours of The Leap and Phantom Spires.

Corey Rich generously let me use his house/office. By the example of his unsurpassed work ethic, I finally felt obligated to stop climbing and actually write this book.

Aidan Maguire gave all of the Wrights Lake information and provided great, detailed feedback.

Once again, Sarah Felchlin pulled together all the text, photos, and maps and then layed them out beautifully.

People who gave first ascent info and beta:
George Connor, Will Cottrell, Paul Crawford, Marek Hajek, Mike Hatchett, Dave Hatchett, Dan Kennedy, Jerry Klatt.

People who sent feedback:
Rob Bell, Charles Booten, John Black, Tony Brake, Dave Buchanan, Gary Carpenter, Eddie Clarke, Alexander Cooper, Bill Cox, Tom DeMint, Brad Jackson, Iztok Marjanovic, Matt Owen, Bill Patrick, Mark Phagan, Michael.Rigney, Pete Ryan, Matthew Schafle, Tad Steele, Jim Thornburg, Mark Tishler, Sasha and Alexandra von Meier, Daniel Wenger, Michael Whitfield, Kevin Willoh, Julianne Young, Dan Zimmerlin.

Past Guidebooks and Authors:
Eric Beck, *Climber's Guide to Lake Tahoe and Donner Summit*, 1973.

Rick Sumner, *A Climber's Guide to Tahoe Rock*, 1980.

Christine Jenkewitz-Meytras, *Tahoe Rock Climbing*, Chockstone Press, 1987.

Mike Carville, *Climber's Guide to Tahoe Rock*, Chockstone Press, 1991.

Mike Carville, *Rock Climbing Lake Tahoe*, Falcon, 1999.

Other Resources:
Sierra Club Bulletin, June, 1954, December 1963, December, 1956.

Wizards of Rock, A History of Free Climbing in America by Pat Ament Wilderness Press, 2002.

– *Chris McNamara*

ACCESS: It's every climber's concern

The Access Fund, a national, non-profit climbers' organization, works to keep climbing areas open and to conserve the climbing environment. Need help with closures? Land acquisition? Legal or land management issues? Funding for trails and other projects? Starting a local climbers' group? CALL US!

Climbers can help preserve access by being committed to leaving the environment in its natural state. Here are some simple guidelines:

• **ASPIRE TO CLIMB WITHOUT LEAVING A TRACE,** especially in environmentally sensitive areas like caves. Chalk can make a significant impact on dark and porous rock—don't use it around historic rock art. Pick up litter, and leave trees and plants intact.

• **DISPOSE OF HUMAN WASTE PROPERLY.** Use toilets whenever possible. If toilets are not available, dig a "cat hole" at least six inches deep and 200 feet from any water, trails, campsites, or the base of climbs. *Always pack out toilet paper.* On big wall routes, use a "poop tube" and carry waste up and off with you (the old "bag toss" is now illegal in many areas).

• **USE EXISTING TRAILS.** Cutting across switchbacks causes erosion. When walking off-trail, tread lightly, especially in the desert where cryptogamic soils (usually a dark crust) take thousands of years to form and are easily damaged. Be aware that "rim ecologies" (the clifftop) are often highly sensitive to disturbance.

• **BE DISCREET WITH FIXED ANCHORS.** *Bolts are controversial and are not a convenience—don't place them unless they are really necessary.* Camouflage all anchors. Remove unsightly slings from rappel stations (better to use steel chain or welded cold shuts). Bolts sometimes can be used proactively to protect fragile resources—consult with your local land manager.

• **RESPECT THE RULES** and speak up when other climbers don't. Expect restrictions in designated wilderness areas, rock art sites, caves, and in sensitive wildlife areas such as nesting sites for birds of prey. *Power drills are illegal in wilderness areas and all national parks.*

• **PARK AND CAMP IN DESIGNATED AREAS.** Some climbing areas require a permit for overnight camping.

• **MAINTAIN A LOW PROFILE.** Leave the boom box and day-glo clothing at home. The less climbers are seen and heard, the better.

• **RESPECT PRIVATE PROPERTY.** Be courteous to land owners. Don't climb where you're not wanted.

• **JOIN THE ACCESS FUND.** To become a member, make a tax-deductible donation of $25.

THE ACCESS FUND
*Keeping climbing areas open and
conserving the climbing environment*
P.O. Box 17010
Boulder, CO 80308

A deadly bolt more than 20 years old ... one of several
thousand on popular climbs throughout the United States.

A new bolt rated to over 5,000 pounds. The ASCA
wants to replace the bad bolt above with one of these.

Bad Bolts Kill

We need YOUR help. The American Safe Climbing Association has helped replace more than
4,500 bolts throughout the country. We estimate that there are more than 20,000 bad bolts
remaining on popular climbs today. Your $50 donation will make at least one route safe . . . and
that one route could be the next one you climb. The ASCA would like to get there before you do.

Does your crag need
re-bolting? Please
contact us.

asca
American Safe Climbing Association

$25 Supporter $50 Contributor $100 Advocate $500 Lifer

Name

Address

E-Mail/Phone

All contributors receive the ASCA newsletter.
Make checks payable to: ASCA, 2 Bradford Way, Mill Valley, CA 94941
or donate online at www.safeclimbing.org

The American Safe Climbing Association is a 501(c)3 organization and contributions are tax-deductible.

Preface

Welcome to another SuperTopo guide. Like our other print books and eBooks, *South Lake Tahoe Climbing* uniquely combines elements that can make your climbing experience a great one: detailed topo, pitch length, gear sizes, strategy, approach and descent maps, needed info on driving, eating and camping, great photos, and climber history.

This book of 184 pages is a jump up from the 40 pages in our *Lover's Leap Select* eBook released two year ago. We think it takes coverage of the Tahoe area up a significant notch. Can we do even better? Sure, and here's where you come in.

We need your corrections, feedback, and suggestions for new routes. The more detailed the feedback, the better. We listen and try to respond to every piece of feedback we get. So don't be shy, send me a note at chris@supertopo.com and let me know which routes should be in the next edition, any errors you noticed in this book, or just general feedback. SuperTopo is very much a personal, human-scale operation and you are an important part of it.

Chris McNamara
Founder/CEO
SuperTopo LLC

The spectacular Eagle Falls above Emerald Bay. (Justin Bailie)

Introduction

George Connor on a 1975 ascent of Farley at Sugarloaf.

Ann Carlson

South Lake Tahoe offers exquisite year-round climbing for every ability and taste. Trad climbers can jam smooth Yosemite-like cracks at Sugarloaf or Eagle Lake, pull on steep knobs at Phantom Spires, lead their first multi-pitch route at Lover's Leap. Sport climbers can clip bolts at Luther Rock, Luther Spires and Mayhem Cove. This book focuses on some of the highest quality granite in the Sierra, but unlike Yosemite's glacier-polished rock, Tahoe granite is more textured with knobs, dikes, and edges. This makes it a little more "user friendly" and means you climb steeper routes at easier grades.

In Tahoe it's easy to change elevations and find a crag with perfect temperatures. Go to Sugarloaf if a cold snap rolls in, switch to Lover's Leap and Phantom Spires in mild conditions, or climb at Eagle Lake Cliff and Wrights Lake Cliff to escape the heat. Good climbing weather is always at hand.

You also get to choose your level of serenity. Eagle Creek Cliff and Wrights Lake Cliff have alpine lakes, craggy peaks, and silence. Lover's Leap or 90-Foot Wall are more social destinations and right by the road. Sit around a fire at the Phantom Spires camping area or go big at the Stateline casinos. Cook ramen on your Whisperlite stove or eat Sushi in South Lake Tahoe. You get to choose.

We all love Yosemite and Tuolumne, but the fact is they're often a logistical hassle. Not so in Tahoe. No advanced planning, no reservations, no fees, and no ranger presence. You camp for free on most Forest Service land and there is always a supermarket, restaurant, or latté nearby.

Joel Booth looking better than average on Pony Express. (Chris McNamara)

Unlike the National Parks, dogs are allowed at all the climbing areas (and can guard your pack from squirrels).

Tahoe is the ideal training ground for Yosemite's long routes. Rather than get bogged down in the crowds on Yosemite's limited selection of 5.6-5.9s, build your skills on Tahoe's more numerous moderates and then head to the Valley. If you live in the Bay Area, most Tahoe crags are closer than Yosemite. For some, Sugarloaf is even closer than Pinnacles.

Gear

The standard Tahoe traditional climbing rack is two sets of cams, 1-2 sets of nuts, 10 quickdraws, and 6-10 slings. A single 60m rope suffices to descend and toprope most climbs. However, for maximum toprope options, use a 70m rope. In rare cases, two ropes are mandatory to descend. When toproping, it's often useful to extend the anchor by 10 feet so the rope doesn't run over an edge. For this purpose, bring 20 feet of webbing or a cordalette. Always carry a hat, gloves, and light jacket in case of a thunderstorm.

On many Lover's Leap climbs, you must carry a lightweight pair of running shoes or approach shoes to walk off the top. Most climbers do not tape their hands for Tahoe routes but it's not a bad idea to bring a roll of 2-inch athletic tape.

Anchor Conditions

Since 1997 the American Safe Climbing Association has replaced more than 200 bolts in Lake Tahoe. Most popular routes have bomber belays and lead bolts. The ASCA has replaced many bad bolts in South Lake Tahoe but many poor bolts remain. For the most up-to-date information on each route's anchor conditions, visit the ASCA web site at: www.safeclimbing.org

When to Climb

Most Tahoe climbing areas have ideal temperatures in the spring and fall. In the summer, seek the shade and climb at the higher elevation crags. Sugarloaf is the only winter crag in this guide. Get more weather detail in the overview for each area.

Getting There

Car Travel
A car is essential in Tahoe as public transportation is scarce. From San Francisco, drive Interstate 80 to Sacramento and join Highway 50. Access all climbing areas in this guide off Highway 50 or Highway 89. Be aware that many people get speeding tickets 10 miles east of Placerville.

Introductory Tahoe Crags

These areas all have climbs in the 5.6-5.9 range:

90-Foot Wall
Phantom Spires
Lover's Leap, Hogsback
Lover's Leap, East Wall
Luther Spires
Echo Lakes

Air Travel
Reno/Tahoe Airport is about an hour drive to South Lake Tahoe and Sacramento International Airport is about two hours away. Rent a car at the airport. You can also fly into Oakland or San Francisco, rent a car and drive about three hours.

Lodging and Motels

Only 5 minutes from Lover's Leap, the Strawberry Lodge offers rooms at $55-110. They also have a good bar. South Lake Tahoe has many motels as well as more upscale hotels near the casinos on the Nevada side of the line.

Camping

In the introduction to each specific climbing area are more details on camping. Most climbers, no matter where they climb, camp at Lover's Leap or Phantom Spires.

Restaurants

Here are our favorite South Lake Tahoe restaurants: **Lake Tahoe Pizza** (1168 Highway 50; 530-544-1919) has good pizza and a salad bar. **Rude Brothers** has good coffee, bagels, and moderate prices. **Izzies Burger Spa** (2591 Lake Tahoe Boulevard; 530-544-5030) offers great burgers and a salad bar. For excellent Mexican food head to **The Cantina** (Highway 89 and 10th Street; 530-544-1233). **Sprouts** (3123 Harrison Avenue; 530-541-6969) has great natural food. **Ernie's** (1146 Emerald Bay Road; 530-541-2161)—a classic greasy spoon—serves a good breakfast. **Naked Fish** (3940 Lake Tahoe Blvd; 530-541-FISH) serves sushi and unique cuisine. The best Thai food is at **Orchid's** (2180 Lake Tahoe Boulevard; 530-544-5541). **Tep's Villa Roma** (530-541-8227) offers good Italian food. If you're craving good franchised coffee, visit **Starbucks** in either Placerville or west of Raley's supermarket on Highway 50. The **Strawberry Lodge,** just a 5-minute walk from The Leap, offers good American food at moderate prices and has a bar. In Pollock Pines, 30 minutes west of The Leap on Highway 50, there is a decent coffee shop called **Pony Espresso**.

A favorite Mexican restaurant for both locals and travelers is **Los Hermanos.** Not surprisingly, it's crowded on weekends. Both Pony Espresso and Los Hermanos are off the Sly Park Road Exit in Pollock Pines.

Groceries

Raley's, located at the junction of 89 and 50 in South Lake Tahoe, offers the best prices and selection. **Liras** (2977 Highway 50; 530-577-5399) located in Meyers, is smaller and little more pricey. If you're staying at Lover's Leap, **Strawberry Market**, located across from Strawberry Lodge, has a small selection of essential items at high prices. If driving from the Bay Area, there are **Safeway** stores in Placerville and Pollack Pines.

Climbing Guides

Lover's Leap Guides (530-318-2939, www.loversleap.net) is a guide service run by some of the most experienced Lover's Leap climbers. They offer classes in beginning to advanced climbing, learning to lead, summiting all the Phantom Spires and adaptive climbing.
  Alpine Skills International (530-582-9170) and **Sierra Mountain Guides** (www.sierramtnguides.com) also offer group trips and private guiding to climbs at Lover's Leap and the rest of the Tahoe area. **Epic Adventures** (408-261-0464, www.climbepic.com) has been guiding since 1977 at Lover's Leap as well as the Pinnacles and Castle Rock.

Climbing Gear

The best selection of gear and climbing beta is at **Sports Ltd.** (530-544-2284) in South Lake Tahoe at the South Y Shopping Center next to Raley's.

Rope Madness

What's up with rope length standards? Five years ago we were all upgraded to 60m ropes. Now 70m ropes are catching on!?

We feel your pain. It does seem a little mad and the whole movement to longer ropes begs the question, "When does it stop? 80m? 90m? Longer?"

A 60m rope suffices for all the climbs in this book. A 70m rope requires extra rope management on multi-pitch climbs and is generally overkill. However, a 70m rope gives you more options to toprope. You don't need to junk that 60m cord. But, if shopping for a new rope, and you do a lot of cragging and toproping, consider 70m.

Rest Days

When you need a rest day or just want to mix things up, consider riding two world-class mountain bike trails: **The Flume Trail** and **Mister Toad's Wild Ride**. In summer, buy a lift ticket to ride at a ski resort. Hike one of the many trails or head for the water of Lake Tahoe to kayak, water ski, or just sit on the beach.
  For guidebooks and recommendations from knowledgeable locals, visit South Lake Tahoe's best outdoor sports shop, **Sports Ltd.** (in South Lake Tahoe at the South Y Shopping Center next to Raley's; 530-544-2284).
  Most of the nightlife is at the Harrah's or Harvey's casinos. In the winter, take the rare opportunity to spend half the day skiing and half the day cragging at Sugarloaf.

Minimizing Impacts

Chris McNamara

All Tahoe climbing areas are on National Forest land and are subject to few restrictions. Let's keep it that way. Fewer environmental impacts and fewer confrontations with rangers and private landowners mean fewer restrictions on our climbing.

The Leave No Trace principles are a good place to start:

- Plan Ahead and Prepare
- Travel and Camp on Durable Surfaces
- Dispose of Waste Properly
- Leave What You Find
- Minimize Campfire Impacts
- Respect Wildlife
- Be Considerate of Other Visitors

If we all abide by these principles, we will be in good shape. But, to really preserve our climbing freedoms, we need to go beyond. Following is a list of things to do and how to get involved:

Be low-key at Lover's Leap Campground

In recent years there have been subtle increases in regulation at the campground. To make sure this trend does not continue, be as low key as possible. Respect the 14 total days per year limit. Put out your campfires. Drive slowly and don't park on the residential road. The less climbers bring attention to themselves, the more freedom they will get.

Organize trail projects to reduce erosion

Trail projects come up every few years at Lover's Leap and can generally use your help. Talk to locals and find out if there is an upcoming project. You can make a difference.

Join the Access Fund

This is a terrific organization that keeps climbing areas open. Members invest their resources in preserving the Tahoe climbing experience and we should invest in them: www.accessfund.org

Join the American Safe Climbing Assn.

ASCA volunteers replace bad anchors and reduce the environmental and visual impacts of anchors. They have replaced anchors at almost every cliff in this guide and need more donations from climbers to continue their work: www.safeclimbing.org

SuperTopo Mission

- Help climbers ascend and descend routes quickly, efficiently, and safely by creating the most accurate and informative climbing topos ever published.

- Capture the mystery, adventure, and humor of climbing by publishing the histories, anecdotes, and outrageous stories of each route.

- Promote clean climbing by publishing the most up-to-date rack info as well as hammerless ratings for each pitch.

- Stress the importance of low impact climbing and promote stewardship of the environment.

Visit www.SuperTopo.com Before Each Climb

There is much more beta available for free on the SuperTopo web site: www.supertopo.com. This information may be more current than the beta available here.

The web site offers additional free beta for each climb:

- photo galleries
- trip reports
- route condition updates
- closures and rockfall warnings
- route beta email alerts

The web site is packed with general South Lake Tahoe info:

- free downloadable color topos
- road and weather conditions
- everything you need to know about staying in Tahoe
- good routes for first-time Tahoe climbers
- general trip planning info

Path to Multi-Pitch Climbing

When you start leading outside, there is a fine line between pushing yourself to improvement and getting in over your head. It is a mark of pride for many climbers that they "started outdoor climbing under-equipped with almost no skills and just winged it." Certainly an essential part of climbing is the personal freedom to push ourselves to our limits. However, get your basic skills dialed before visiting a popular climbing area. You will have more fun and so will the people around you. When you get in over your head at a popular climbing area, you're more likely to drop gear on other climbers, shout back and forth more than necessary, slow down other parties, and put yourself at risk.

Below is a short road map to improving your climbing skills:

Toproping

The path to multi-pitch climbing starts by mastering the basics at a crag where you can toprope. Build a lot of toprope anchors and have an experienced climber critique each one. While on toprope, build crack and face technique and push yourself to see just how hard you can climb. The best toproping areas are 90-Foot Wall, Phantom Spires, Dental Wall and West Buttress at Sugarloaf.

Single Pitch Leading

Start by following many gear leads with an experienced climber. Study the gear placements and pay attention to the use of slings to avoid rope drag.

Next, find a climb that is not heavily used and do numerous "mock leads" where you place gear as if you were leading but also have a toprope. Alternate between cleaning your own gear and having an experienced climber critique your gear placements.

After ten or so mock leads, you are ready to lead single pitch routes that are a few number grades below your toprope ability (if you can toprope 5.9 then start leading 5.6 or easier). Good areas in this guide to lead one-pitch climbs are Phantom Spires, Luther Spires, and Echo Lakes.

Multi-Pitch Leading

Like single-pitch leading, the first step in multi-pitch leading is to follow numerous leads by a more experience climber. Study the systems: rope management, belay organization, and anchor set-up. When you are finally ready to lead a multi-pitch climb, here are some good areas at Lover's Leap to start: Hogsback, Lower Buttress and East Wall.

While this process can be learned on your own, the fastest way to improve is to team up with more experienced climbers or a guide. There are numerous guides for the Tahoe area listed in the Introduction (see page 15).

Crag Comparison

Crag	Page	Number of routes at each grade								Summary
		5.0-5.5	5.6	5.7	5.8	5.9	5.10	5.11	5.12-5.13	
Sugarloaf	25		1	4	6	11	23	12	11	Great Yosemite training. Tahoe's best winter crag.
Phantom Spires	46	2	2	6	10	7	20	19	3	Perfect mixture of face and crack routes.
Wrights Lake	74						8	8	3	Challenging cracks and face in a beautiful setting.
Lover's Leap, East Wall	88			3	5	4	3	1		Incredible selection of 3-4 pitch 5.7-5.10 climbs.
Lover's Leap, Central Wall	96			1	1		2	1		Escape from East Wall crowds. Adventurous climbing.
Lover's Leap, Main Wall/West Wall	101			2		2	6	7	1	Some of The Leap's best short and long routes.
Dear John Buttress	108				2		2	7	3	Steep 5.10-5.12 cracks. Great on hot or rainy days.
Lover's Leap, Lower Buttress	112	1		1	2		5	4		Everything from hard sport to moderate multi-pitch.
Hogwild	118		1	1	2	3	1			Short approach to good quality cracks and face.
Hogsback, North Side	123	2	3	1	1	1				Best intro to multi-pitch climbing in Tahoe.
Lover's Leap, The Box	126							4	2	Stout cracks and face climbs. Secluded from Leap.
Gangsta Wall	134		1		4	1	2		1	Great intro to face and crack climbing. Boat taxi.
Old Peculiar	138			1	1	2	2	3	1	Steep and stout cracks and face.
Berkeley Camp	140					1	1	2	2	A few high-quality sport climbs. Short approach.
Luther Rock	142					1	6	10	1	Great 5.10-5.11 sport climbs.
Luther Spires	146			4	3	3	10	2		Great introduction to sport climbing.
Eagle Lake Cliff	152		1		3	3	15	7	1	Concentrated collection of high quality steep cracks.
Eagle Creek Cliff	160						7	2		Cracks of similar quality and difficulty to Eagle Lake Cliff.
Eagle's Nest	162						4	2	3	Training area for hard, thin cracks. Easy to toprope.
Mayhem Cove	164					1	2	7	8	Fun sport climbing. Mostly 5.11 and harder.
90-Foot Wall	168	3	1	1	1	2	6	4		Great toproping spot. Convenient and crowded.

Free Climbing Ratings

USA Yosemite Decimal System	UIAA	France	UK	Australia
5.1	I	1	M	4
5.2	II	2	D	6
5.3	III / III+	2+	3A/3B VD	8
5.4	IV	3-	3B/3C HVD	
5.5	IV+	3		10
5.6	V-	3+	3C/4A S	12
5.7	V	4	4A/4C VS ; 4A/4B HS	14
5.8	V+	4+		16
5.9	VI-	5	4C/5B HVS	18
5.10a	VI	5+		
5.10b	VI+	6A	5A/5C E1	19
5.10c	VII-	6A+	5B/6A E2	20
5.10d	VII	6B	5C/6A E3	21
5.11a	VII+	6B+		
5.11b	VIII-	6C		22
5.11c		6C+	6A/6B E4	23
5.11d	VIII	7A		24
5.12a	VIII+	7A+	6A/6C E5	
5.12b	IX-	7B		25
5.12c	IX	7B+	6B/6C E6	26
5.12d		7C		27
5.13a	IX+	7C+		28
5.13b	X-	8A	6C/7A E7	29
5.13c	X	8A+		30
5.13d		8B	6C/7A E8	31
5.14a	X+	8B+		32
5.14b	XI-	8C	7A/7B E9	33
5.14c	XI	8C+		34
5.14d	XI+	9A	7A/7B E10	35
5.15a		9A+		36

SUPERTOPO

Cam Sizes by Brand

Ref Size*	BD Camalots	CCH Aliens	Metolius Cams	Trango Big Bros	Wild Country Friends
0.4"	.1 red	.33 black	00 gray		
0.5"	.2 yellow	.375 blue	0 purple		0 red
0.6"	.3 purple	.5 green	1 blue		.5 orange
0.75"	.4 gray	.75 yellow	2 yellow		1 yellow
1"	.5 pink	1 red	3 orange		1.25 brown
1.25"	.75 green	1.5 orange	4 red		1.5 sky
1.5"	1 red	2 purple	5 black		2 pink
1.75"	1 red	2.5 gray	6 green		2.5 royal
2"	2 yellow	2.5 gray	7 blue		3 navy
2.5"	2 yellow		8 purple		3.5 purple
3"	3 blue		9 burgundy		4 black
3.5"	3.5 gray		10 dark blue		4 black
3.5-4.5"	4 purple			1 red	5 silver
4.5-5.5"	4.5 red			2	
5.5-7"	5 green			3 green	6 plum
7-8"				3 green	
8-12"				4 blue	

*"Ref size" is the optimal crack width for a given camming unit. It is not the range given by the manufacturer.

Understanding the Maps

Topo Symbols

Right-facing corner		Roof	⊥⊥⊥⊥	Bolt	x
Left-facing corner		Ledge	⊤⊤⊤⊤	Rappel anchor	
		Slab	///		
Straight-in crack		Belay station	❶	Face climbing	
Groove		Pitch length	130' ●	Pine tree	
Arête				Oak-like tree	
Flake		Optional belay	○	Bush	
				Knob	○
Chimney		False belay	⊘	Hole	●

Notes on Rack

- "nuts" refers to any nut, stopper, or chock. "micro"= #1, 2; "sml"= #3-5; "med"= #6-8; "lrg"= #9-13
- for cams, "2 ea .75-1.5" means bring two sets of all sizes between .75" and 1.5". Check the cam size chart to see which cam corresponds to which crack size.

Notes on Topo

- "belay takes .6-1" means, while leading the pitch, save enough .6-1" cams and nuts to build a natural anchor.
- a number next to a tree is its height.

Topo Abbreviations

ow = offwidth
lb = lieback
p = fixed piton
R = runout (dangerous fall)

Metric System Conversions

1 inch = 2.54 centimeters
1 foot = 0.305 meters
100 feet = 30.5 meters
50 yards = 45.7 meters

Overview Graphics

Canyon Wall	
2WD/4WD dirt road	
Road or State Route	⑩
Federal Highway	⑩
Hikers' trail	
Climbers' trail	
Cross-country travel	

Star Ratings

★★★★★ - undisputed classic
★★★★ - excellent climb
★★★ - good climb
★★ - okay climb
★ - barely included in this book

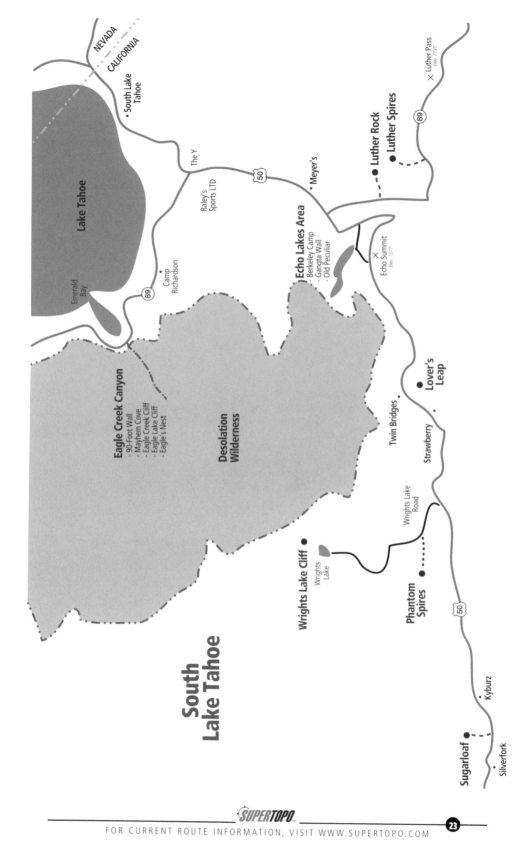

South Lake Tahoe

NEVADA
CALIFORNIA

Lake Tahoe

South Lake Tahoe

Luther Pass
Elev 7735

× Luther Pass

Luther Rock
● Luther Spires

89

The Y

50

Meyer's

Raley's Sports LTD

Echo Lakes Area
- Berkeley Camp
- Gangta Wall
- Old Peculiar

Camp Richardson

Emerald Bay

89

× Echo Summit
Elev 7377

Eagle Creek Canyon
- 90-Foot Wall
- Mayhem Cove
- Eagle Creek Cliff
- Eagle Lake Cliff
- Eagle's Nest

Desolation Wilderness

Lover's Leap ●

Twin Bridges

Strawberry

Wrights Lake Road

Wrights Lake Cliff ●
Wrights Lake

Phantom Spires ●

50

Sugarloaf ●

Kyburz ●

Silverfork

Sugarloaf

Sugarloaf offers Tahoe's best winter cragging. Rising 350 feet out of a steep south-facing slope, it is part spire, part buttress, part dome, and all loaf. The rock has more in common with Yosemite than Phantom Spires or Lover's Leap. Smooth and cleanly fractured features are more common than the knobs, dikes, or big edges that characterize most other Tahoe rock. A dozen major crack and chimney systems stretch two to three pitches from ground to summit. Between these are steep face climbs with thin and positive edges between occasional knobs.

Most face routes have bolts every 5-10 feet. Some are well protected and some a bit scary, but few are runout or dangerous. Delicate smears and edges demand more balance than strength. Sugarloaf 5.10s humble many 5.11 sport climbers. Bring at least a 5.8 leader to get up the moderate classics and a 5.9 or better leader to get a larger sampling of the climbs. There are few 5.4-5.7 routes.

The name "Sugarloaf" refers to the main Sugarloaf formation previously described and the greater Sugarloaf area that includes many 40 to 80-foot-tall boulders nearby. These boulders offer the best toproping opportunities but generally have rock that is more flaky and dirty.

The routes are concentrated; you can lead an easier climb and easily toprope a nearby harder climb. Toprope most climbs with one 60m rope. Most anchors have bolts with chains for rappel.

Getting There

Sugarloaf sits above Highway 50 between Kyburz and Silverfork. It's about 2.5 hours from San Francisco, 30 minutes east of Placerville, and 30 minutes west of South Lake Tahoe. It's about 1.5 hours closer to the Bay Area than Yosemite and consequently day trips are common.

From the west (Placerville), drive .4 miles past the Unocal gas station in Silver Fork and park on the right (south) side of the road in a dirt pullout across from a phone company building.

Chris McNamara

opposite: Mark Leffler traverses Under the Big Top (5.10d), Lover's Leap. (PatittuciPhoto)

From the east (South Lake Tahoe), drive 0.6 miles past Kyburz and park in the dirt pullout on the left (south) side of the road across from a phone company building.

The GPS Coordinate for the Sugarloaf Parking Area: 38° 46' 295", 120° 18' 440"

Please respect local residents by not parking at the school, on Sugarloaf Avenue, or anywhere except for the shoulder of Highway 50.

Approach

The approach for Sugarloaf is a steep and strenuous uphill hike of 25-30 minutes with 700 feet of elevation gain. The approaches for Sugarbun and all other large boulders and outcroppings are shorter.

Start behind the phone company building. Follow a climbers' trail up and right, through a split boulder, then cut up and left. (It's more direct to hike a dirt road just west of the phone company building but this is private property). From here, the trail merges into an old 4WD road and goes straight uphill for 100 yards before turning back to a trail. See the overview map to locate each climb and formation.

When to Climb

Sugarloaf is ideal from October to April and okay from May to September. Various parts of Sugarloaf face east, south, and west, which means there is always something in the sun or shade. The trees buffer most of the wind.

Check the Kyburz weather forecast for current conditions: www.weather.com/weather/local/USCA0559

December–February

A crisp winter day at Sugarloaf can be exceptional. Snow rarely stays longer than a day after a storm except after the occasional big and cold storm. Expect daytime temps in the 50s. Warm up with the morning sun on the East Face in the morning and follow the sun to the West Face in the afternoon.

March–May

Spring brings perfect temps in the shade and warm temps in the sun. Storms can be just as fierce as in the winter but the climbs usually dry quickly.

June–August

Summers are usually too hot. You may find bearable conditions in the morning and afternoons in the shade. However, it's better to just go climbing at higher elevations.

September–November

September usually has a few hot weeks before temperatures cool down and become perfect by October. The first winter storms usually arrive in mid to late November, at which point you may need to climb in the sun to keep warm.

Camping

The nearest camping is at Sand Flat, just west of the Silverfork Unocal 76 gas station. It is a fee area. There is also camping on the Silverfork Road just east of Kyburz which has Forest Service campgrounds (pay fee) and Forest Service land (free). You can also camp at Phantom Spires (see page 48) or Lover's Leap (see page 83).

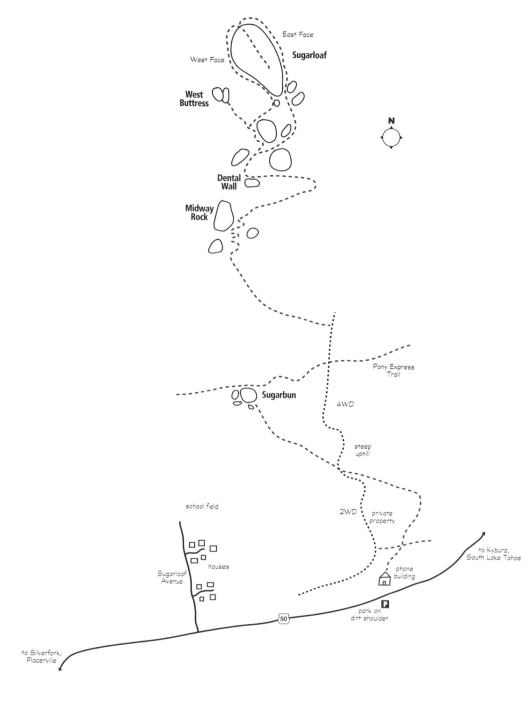

Sugarbun

Approach time: **5 minutes**

Sun exposure: **partial all day**

Height of routes: **50–90'**

This large teardrop-shaped boulder has the
shortest approach and offers two quality
routes among many mediocre ones. It's the
most wind-sheltered Sugarloaf crag. The
dirty and runout 5.7 Flytrap is the easiest
way to set a toprope on other climbs but
most people feel more comfortable leading
Fingerlock (5.10b) to establish topropes.
It's located about halfway between the road
and the main Sugarloaf formation, a few
hundred feet west of the main approach
trail.

Chris McNamara

A. Fingerlock   5.10b★★★

FA: Jim Orey, 1972.

Well-protected, sharp, and sustained
fingercrack. The crux start has powerful
liebacking and fingerlocks with a tree for
feet. (Belayers: spot the leader for the first
10 feet.)

B. Make That Move Now Baby 5.10d★★★★

FA: M. Stumpf, B. Albonico, 1981.

This quality climb involves just about every
face technique. Thin friction crux, then
pull a roof on edges and sidepulls to an
exhilarating arête finish. Bring long slings
to toprope.

C. Fly Trap   5.7 R★★

FA: unknown

Climb a chimney to the top of a huge flake,
then dirty face. Runout and scary for the
grade.

D. Mad Dog   5.10d★★

FA: unknown

Short, steep, and powerful fingerlock crux
to easier climbing. Maybe worth toproping.

E. Dog Fight   5.11c★★

FA: Al Swanson, John Nye.

Edges amidst the moss. At the third bolt,
make a desperate move left to the crack.
Toprope from the Make That Move Now
Baby anchor. (Use long slings to reduce
ropedrag.)

F. Dirty Dog   5.10b★★

FA: unknown

Friction, edges, and mantels on a somewhat
dirty face. Use the Fingerlock anchor to set
a toprope.

G. Wintergreen   5.10c★★

FA: Paul Crawford, Jay Smith.

Interesting sidepulls and edges on the arête.
A little runout on 5.7 after the third bolt.
Named after Wintergreen snuff that the
rock seems to be plastered with.

A. Fingerlock 5.10b★★★★ cams: 2 ea .5-1.5"

B. Make That Move Now Baby 5.10d★★★★ 9 draws

C. Fly Trap 5.7 R★★ cams: 1 ea .5-4"

D. Mad Dog 5.10d★★ cams: 1 ea .4-2"

E. Dog Fight 5.11c★★ cams: 1 ea .5-1", 3 draws

F. Dirty Dog 5.10b★★ 3 draws

G. Wintergreen 5.10c★★ 3 draws

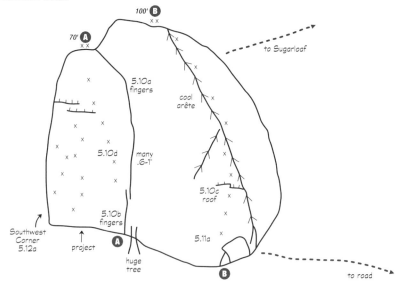

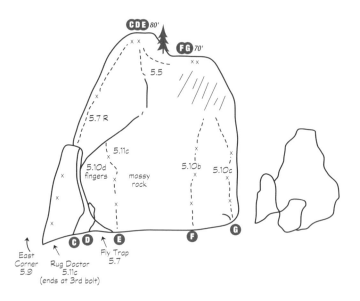

Midway Rock

Approach time: **15 minutes**

Sun exposure: **afternoon**

Height of routes: **30–60'**

Midway Rock is located on the trail halfway between Sugarbun and Sugarloaf. It's easy to get to the top and establish topropes. However, there are only a few good climbs and all of them are challenging and a little awkward. As a result, this rock is rarely climbed.

A. Flight Deck   5.11c★★

FA: Blair Haffly, Paul Brown, 1985.

Thin and desperate face moves. Easy to toprope.

B. Self Abuse   5.10b★★★

FA: Royal Robbins, 1967.

This burly offwidth is easy to toprope and a convenient way to learn the craft of flared, overhanging slots—if that's your thing. There is a high bolt anchor and a low bolt anchor for toproping; use the lower bolts.

C. The Diagonal, Left   5.9★★

FA: unknown

A short and stout climb with sustained 5.9 hands and offwidth. Tight hands start widens to fist then an awkward wide move at the top. Natural anchor.

D. The Diagonal, Right   5.9★

FA: unknown

Strenuous undercling right (get a good spot from belayer) leads to an awkward squeeze/bulge. Not the best rock. 1-1.5" for anchor.

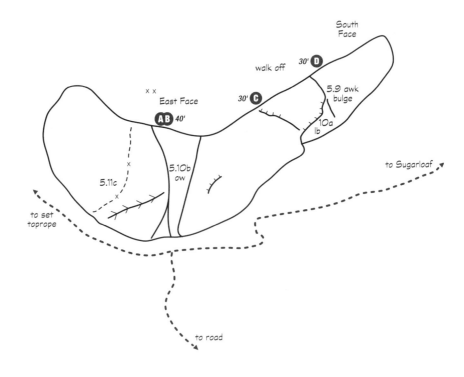

Dental Wall

Approach time: **15 minutes**

Sun exposure: **afternoon**

Height of routes: **30–60'**

These climbs are extremely convenient to toprope as the main approach trail passes within feet of the anchors. There is usually just one bolt above each climb—make sure to incorporate two bolts to each anchor (don't belay off just one!). Good warmup climbs. All climbs only get two stars because of the flaky rock. These climbs are a convenient way to practice thin edging and friction technique.

A. Cracked Tooth 5.8★★ must be led

B. Gumline 5.9★★

C. Cuspid 5.6★★

D. Plumbline 5.10d★★

E. Toothpick 5.10d★★

F. Gingivitis 5.10d★★

Chris McNamara

South Face

Approach time: 25 minutes

Sun exposure: morning to afternoon

Height of routes: 200–350'

The South Face offers a few sunny climbs in an exceptionally exposed position. To descend, rappel the routes or climb to the top of Sugarloaf via Harding's Chimney.

A. Harder Than It Used To Be   5.12a★★★

FA: John Scott.

5.12a thin hard boulder problem. Easy to toprope after climbing Pitch 1 of Bolee Gold.
Rack: 7 draws

B. Bolee Gold   5.10c★★★★★

FA: Garry Anderson, Jay Smith, and Rick Sumner, 1977.

Bolee Gold climbs a proud arête/buttress and is the most aesthetic and continuously exposed line on Sugarloaf. The climbing involves crimping and smearing on a featured face covered in good edges and small knobs. It is well-protected on the 5.10 sections and runout on 5.8 and easier terrain. This was the first free route to reach the South Summit.

The first pitch climbs steep edges and is the most sustained and best protected. The second pitch is the crux and has thin and tricky face moves at the third bolt. There are a few gear placements and knob tieoffs on the second part of this pitch. There are

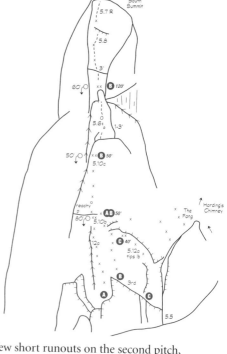

a few short runouts on the second pitch, which warm you up for the longer runouts on Pitch 3. This third pitch is a gem with knobs and big exposure to a cool summit. There are a few mediocre knob tieoffs and a horizontal crack that augment the scanty three bolts.

Many climbers do the route in two long pitches by using the optional bolted anchor after the crux on the second pitch. Rappel the route with one 60m rope or rappel into the notch on the north side of the summit and continue up the last pitch of Harding's Chimney.
Rack: cams: 1 ea .75-1.5", 1 ea 3.5"; 6 draws

C. Hooker's Haven   5.12a★★★★

FA: Jim Orey, Charlie Jones, 1971 and 1972.
FFA: Mark Hudon, Max Jones, 1978.

This old aid route—once rated 5.9 A4—got its name from the wild A4 hooking between the arch and what today is the first belay of Bolee Gold (an anchor was later added at the end of the arch). The route was one of the first 5.12s at Sugarloaf and freed with EBs. You can't pull through it on bolts.
Rack: 4 draws

Chris McNamara

opposite: Tommy Caldwell on Grand Illusion (5.13c). (PatitucciPhoto)

East Face

Approach time: **25 minutes**

Sun exposure: **morning to early afternoon**

Height of routes: **200–350'**

The East Face offers the highest concentration of quality climbs at The Loaf. Every 20 feet along the base there is a classic crack or face climb ranging from one to three pitches. Most climbers warm up on Farley or Dominion, then move to harder routes.

Descent

Descend most routes by rappelling. For routes that end on the Middle Summit, walk north down mostly 3rd class with a few brief 4th class moves (including a brief tree downclimb). A climbers' trail contours back to the base.

D. The Fang   5.9★★★

FA: Jim Orey, M. Vincent, 1971.

A cruxy tight hands section low leads into a cool chimney. Place gear high in the chimney and make an awkward but fun exit to the outside. Rappel from the top of The Fang or continue up Harding's Chimney.

E. Bird Man   5.11d★★★★★

FA: unknown

Heads up but not runout. Sustained, technical, thin face with three 5.11 cruxes. Elegant, rewarding, good position. Bring a second rope to rappel. Tricky pro at start.

F. Talking Heads   5.11b★★★

FA: Jay Smith, Paul Crawford, 1982.

Tenuous face moves after the first bolt leads to juggier and more moderate terrain. Usually toproped. This route, and many others at the cliff, are named after 80s rock. Tricky pro at start.

G. Stone   5.10a R★★

FA: Greg Dexter, Steve Miller, 1976.

Usually toproped after climbing first half of the first pitch of Harding's Chimney. The 5.10d variation starts out of the tree.

The crux involves steep and reachy knob climbing. Sling knobs for extra protection.

H. South Summit Bolt Ladder   5.10a★★

FA: Warren Harding.

If climbing Harding's Chimney or Scheister, take a short detour and tag the south summit (the coolest Sugarloaf summit). Most climbers just pull through the tricky 5.10a crux using quickdraws (no aiders necessary).

I. Harding's Chimney   5.8★★★★

FA: Warren Harding, John Ohrenschall, 1954.

This is a classic old-school route for three reasons: it takes an obvious line, involves some spooky chimney climbing, and was put up by Warren Harding. The first pitch is the psychological and physical crux and features 5.8 squeeze chimney with a 50-foot runout (can be protected with 9-10" pieces). The second and third pitches are much more moderate and well-protected. The third pitch has a brief section of 5.7 face before an easy gully to a notch. Belay here and then do a short tunnel-through to the west side. For an alternate finish, stay on the east side and take the intimidating 5.8 stemming finish (look for the bolt and move right). Walk off to descend.

J. Gallows Pole   5.11b★★★★

FA: Paul Crawford, Rick Van Horn, 1982.

Climb the first 20 feet of Harding's Chimney and traverse right. Sustained 5.11a knob moves up high. Easy to toprope with one 60m rope after climbing the first pitch of Harding's Chimney. 5.11d direct bolted start by Joel Moore.

K. Beast of Burden   5.12a★★★

FA: Chris Clifford, et al, 1984.

Bewildering opening moves ease to sustained 5.10 arête climbing. Usually toproped by rappelling from bolts near first belay of Harding's Chimney.

L. Scheister   5.7★★★★

FA: unknown

This route rivals Harding's Chimney in quality and difficulty. The crux first pitch starts with steep broken rock (stem when possible) before entering a smooth flared chimney. Stay outside (where the chimney is wider) and occasionally reach in to place gear. This pitch protects better than Harding's Chimney but is still only recommended for confident 5.7 leaders. The second pitch has a great mixture of 5.7 hand jams and lieback moves and ends at a notch. From here, climb the third pitch of Harding's Chimney to the middle summit. Walk off to descend.

M. Blue Velvet   5.10c★★★★

FA: Will Cottrell.

If you climb all three pitches, this route is almost as good as Bolee Gold. Most climbers just do the first pitch because the second and third pitches are bold. On the first pitch, a tricky start leads to sustained 5.9 and 5.10 moves. The bolts are far enough apart to get your attention. Toprope the first pitch (barely!) with a 60m rope but only if the belayer moves up the ramp at the start of Scheister (be careful!).

The second pitch is also fun but rarely led as it involves a big runout on 5.8 face followed by tricky 5.10c face moves. Set up a toprope on the second pitch by climbing Scheister. You can then easily rappel down and set a toprope on the first pitch.

The exhilarating third pitch is runout on 5.8 and 5.9 moves but well-protected at the 5.10 moves at the top. From the last belay, move over to the last 20 feet of Harding's Chimney.

N. Crushed Velvet   5.10c★★★★

FA: Aidan Maguire, Scott Bye, 1998.

As good as Blue Velvet but with more sustained moves and a little more distance between bolts. Down low, climb right of the bolts and use the arête/corner when possible. Bring medium cams for the Farley start and a few nuts and a .6" cam for an optional gear placement up high. When finished, traverse into Farley and go to the summit or rappel to the Blue Velvet anchor and toprope that climb or rappel 100 feet to Opus 7.

Chris McNamara

O. Farley   5.9★★★★

FA: Eric Beck, Steve Roper, mid-60s;
Knobby Wall finish: Jim Orey, 1971.

The first pitch, an incredible lieback flake,
is easily the best 5.9 at Sugarloaf. This
sustained pitch has just a few footholds. The
second pitch climbs a chimney that fades to
tricky corner and then back to a chimney.
The third pitch ascends a flared corner onto
the awesome and runout Knobby Wall.
Most climbers just do the first pitch. Only
recommended for confident 5.9 leaders.

P. Opus 7   5.11d★★★

FA: Paul Crawford and Jay Smith, 1987.

Extremely thin and technical face moves
that are unrelenting after the third bolt. The
second pitch is runout and rarely climbed.
(Actually, it was part of the first pitch until
someone retro-bolted it.) Usually toproped
after climbing the first pitch of Farley.
Named after the symphony.

Q. Grand Illusion   5.13c★★★★★

FA: Ken Edsberg, Jack Davidson, 9/63.
FFA: Tony Yaniro, 1979.

With an average angle of 135 degrees,
this is the most spectacular and difficult
crack climb in Tahoe. After an initial
boulder problem, the route ascends power
endurance locks and stemming to a tricky
finish. There are many fixed nuts.

This pitch was first aid climbed in 1963
as a variation to Harding's Chimney. The
first ascent took five hours and required
18 pitons, some of which might still be
in the rock. The first free ascent came 16
years later and was named Grand Illusion.
At the time it was not only the hardest
free climb in the world, it was the world's
first 5.13. Tony Yaniro described the route
as "straightforward and just hard." He
built crack simulators to train for the
route and used the emerging technique of
hangdogging to boulder the moves. He led
the route with pre-placed gear in EBs. In
1988 Hidetaka Suzuki made the first and
still only lead without pre-placed gear.

R. The Mini Illusion   5.12b★★★

FA: still a project.

A pumpy and technical journey under a
massive roof. The thin crux involves belly
crawling on a vertical wall with thin finger
locks and few footholds. The route has
permanent draws; lower from anywhere.

S. Taurus   5.11b★★★★

FA: Mark Hudon, Max Jones, 1976.

Sharp locks for 15 feet, then sustained
and pumpy 5.10 liebacking. Stem when
possible. A great toprope after climbing The
Fracture and great for building endurance.
The second pitch wanders up a runout face
up and left of Silver Ledge and is rarely
climbed. A variation to the second pitch
called Lady Luck goes straight up after the
first bolt on runout terrain. There's a bolt
up there somewhere. This was the first 5.11
climb in the Tahoe area and only two years
later first ascensionist Mark Hudon free
soloed it.

T. The Fracture   5.10d★★★★

FA: unknown

The most classic Sugarloaf finger crack.
Lieback start leads to finger jams with few
footholds. The crux involves powerful pulls
between good locks. The original route
continues two more pitches to the summit.
The second pitch has some dangerous loose
flakes and is rarely climbed. The third pitch
was an old aid pitch that was free climbed
and renamed Grand Illusion.

U. Telesis   5.11b★★★★

FA: Jay Smith, Paul Crawford, 1987.

Unrelenting thin face moves from the first
bolt to the last. Mostly well protected but
potential for big falls near the top. Usually
toproped after climbing Dominion. Was
originally called Swamp Thing. Many bolts
were added after the first ascent.

V. Dominion   5.10a★★★★

FA: Gene Drake, Dan Hart, Jim Orey, 1972.

Great way to break into 5.10. Well-protected and mostly 5.8 and 5.9 hand jamming to a 5.10a lieback and stemming crux. Descend to the ground by rappelling from the bolt anchors on the right with a 60m rope or rappel from the left bolt anchors and toprope Telesis.

W. Captain Fingers   5.12c★★★★

FA: Gene Drake, Jim Hicks, 1970.
FFA: Mark Hudon, Max Jones 1979.

Thin locks and powerful liebacking on beautiful green lichen-splotched granite. The gear is tiny and challenging to place on lead until after the crux when you reach a bomber hand jam and a 3.5" cam. Usually toproped after climbing Dominion.

X. Morticia   5.9★★★

FA: Aidan Maguire, Don Bradley, 2000.

A fun mixture of crack and face that is more mental than physical. The first crux comes moving left around a roof (stay low and left). The second crux comes a few bolts up on the face. You can barely toprope this climb with a 60m rope but the belayer may need to walk up the gully a little ways.

Y. Lurch   5.8 R★★★

FA: Jim Hicks, Larry Morris, 1971.

Start up the same corner as Morticia but move right out the roof to a bolt and then the chain anchor. The second pitch is runout but mostly 5.6 or easier knob climbing. The last 20 feet are mossy and require some routefinding. The first pitch is easily toproped with a 60m rope.

Chris McNamara psyching himself up for the crux of Harding's Chimney. (Pierre De St Croix)

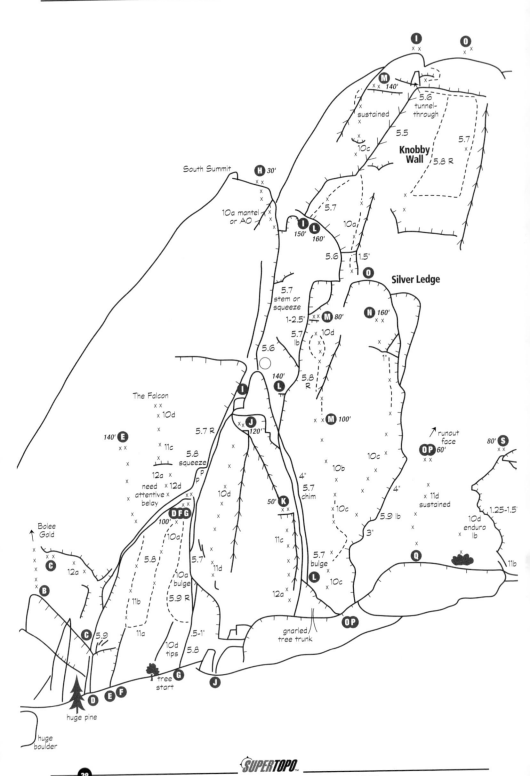

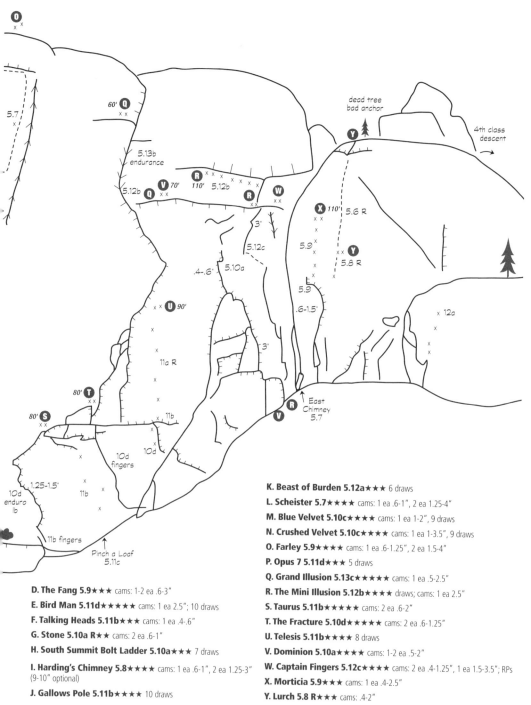

K. **Beast of Burden 5.12a**★★★ 6 draws

L. **Scheister 5.7**★★★★ cams: 1 ea .6-1", 2 ea 1.25-4"

M. **Blue Velvet 5.10c**★★★★ cams: 1 ea 1-2", 9 draws

N. **Crushed Velvet 5.10c**★★★★ cams: 1 ea 1-3.5", 9 draws

O. **Farley 5.9**★★★★ cams: 1 ea .6-1.25", 2 ea 1.5-4"

P. **Opus 7 5.11d**★★ 5 draws

Q. **Grand Illusion 5.13c**★★★★★ cams: 1 ea .5-2.5"

R. **The Mini Illusion 5.12b**★★★★ draws; cams: 1 ea 2.5"

S. **Taurus 5.11b**★★★★ cams: 2 ea .6-2"

T. **The Fracture 5.10d**★★★★ cams: 2 ea .6-1.25"

U. **Telesis 5.11b**★★★ 8 draws

V. **Dominion 5.10a**★★★ cams: 1-2 ea .5-2"

W. **Captain Fingers 5.12c**★★★ cams: 2 ea .4-1.25", 1 ea 1.5-3.5"; RPs

X. **Morticia 5.9**★★★ cams: 1 ea .4-2.5"

Y. **Lurch 5.8 R**★★★ cams: .4-2"

D. **The Fang 5.9**★★★ cams: 1-2 ea .6-3"

E. **Bird Man 5.11d**★★★★★ cams: 1 ea 2.5"; 10 draws

F. **Talking Heads 5.11b**★★★ cams: 1 ea .4-.6"

G. **Stone 5.10a R**★★ cams: 2 ea .6-1"

H. **South Summit Bolt Ladder 5.10a**★★★ 7 draws

I. **Harding's Chimney 5.8**★★★★ cams: 1 ea .6-1", 2 ea 1.25-3"
(9-10" optional)

J. **Gallows Pole 5.11b**★★★★ 10 draws

West Face

Approach time: **25 minutes**

Sun exposure: **noon to sunset**

Height of routes: **200'**

The West Face doesn't have nearly the concentration of classic routes as the East Face but there are a few gems. There are a few good topropes, but establishing them usually requires a little extra effort.

A. Ziplock   5.11d★★

FA: Aidan Maguire, John Robinson, 2001.

Starting from the top of Bolee Gold's first pitch, Ziplock makes a 90-foot 11d horizontal traverse to the left.

B. The Ghost in the Machine   5.12a★★★★

FA: Ed Drummond, Mark Robinson, 1984.

This is the longest hard route at Sugarloaf. Well-protected cruxes between some runout faces. Third pitch is heads up. Use double ropes on the fourth pitch.

Blindfaith (not shown)   5.9★★★

FA: Jim Orey, John Bowlin, Charley Jones, 1973.

From the first belay of Fat Merchant Crack, climb up left into a steep, left-facing corner. Higher, at a roof, hand traverse out right and join the third pitch of Bolee Gold. WARNING: This climb has a dangerously sharp edge near the start of the traverse. If the follower falls on the starting moves, the rope can slide down an arête and cut through. One fatality and at least one known near-fatal accident have occurred.

C. Sugar Daddy   5.11c★★★★

FA: Joel Moore, 1992.

The first pitch is an excellent and well-protected 5.11c. Chimney up Fat Merchant crack, then step right, clip a bolt, and climb a stalactite (optional .5" cam). Second pitch is 5.12a thin face and rarely climbed. Shares second pitch of Ghost in the Machine.

D. Fat Merchant's Crack   5.10a X★★★

FA: TM Herbert, Royal Robbins, 1967.

Sugarloaf's wide crack testpiece. After 50 feet, the chimney narrows to a leaning, unprotected 5.10a offwidth. After the crux, place big gear and clip a hidden piton. Belay on a sloping ledge. On the second pitch, a difficult flared corner leads to 5.7 face to the south notch. Continue up the last pitch of Harding's Chimney. Way scarier than Twilight Zone in Yosemite or Easy Wind in Tuolumne Meadows.

E. Grand Delusion   5.12d★★★★

FA: Chris Clifford.

Originally a 5.8 A2 route called Scapegoat. Technical, tricky, sustained, and a little harder than Captain Fingers. Good aid practice. Can toprope after climbing Pan Dulce.

F. TM's Deviation   5.10a★★★★

FA: TM Herbert, Bruce Cooke, 1968.

This intimidating climb involves some grueling overhanging chimneys, fist cracks, and hand cracks. Do the first pitch of West Chimney (5.5) for about 80 feet. A short and easy traverse pitch to the right leads to a beautiful gold-polished left-facing dihedral. Liebacking, jamming, and offwidth brings you to a short and strenuous fingers lieback then a belay. A short and easy pitch leads you to the top.

G. West Chimney   5.8★★

FA: Warren Harding, John Ohrenschall, 6/53.

The first ascent of this climb was actually a miscalculated attempt to reach the south summit of Sugarloaf. Harding and Ohrenschall failed to reach the unclimbed south summit from the east face so they moved their efforts to the west face. Starting in the afternoon, they climbed the first 240 feet with only two pitons for protection and decided to bivy for the night on the rock. The next morning they faced the crux where it's not clear what they did. According to Ohrenschall, "After seven tries, we decided to resort to the unorthodox method of prusiking in order to surmount this obstacle." Past the crux they scrambled up 3rd and 4th class rock to the main Sugarloaf summit where they realized they missed the south summit by almost 200 feet. In his account of the climb Ohrenschall gave this advice to future climbers: "With three men, the leader can be given a shoulder stand in perfect safety; this will put him in a good position to use hardware on the chief obstacle of the climb."

H. Expresso   5.11a★★★

FA: Joel Moore.

Climb the first pitch of Pony Express, then head straight up on five or so bolts. A little heads up but not runout. Descend by rapping back to Pony Express.

I. Cry Uncle   5.12a R★★★

FA: Bill Todd, 1977 and 1978.
FFA: Tom Herbert, Paul Crawford, 1987.

A spooky lead or fun toprope after climbing Pony Express. Good edges with bad feet lead to balancy diagonal crack. 5.10 tips lieback with mediocre nuts and occasional cams for pro. Be careful—some flakes are fragile.

J. Pony Express   5.8★★★★

FA: (Pitch 1) Dick Long, mid-1960s;
(Pitch 2) Gene Drake, Jim Hicks, 1970.

The first pitch is the best 5.8 at Sugarloaf. Sustained hand jams and lieback on perfect rock. Great for laps on toprope. The second pitch is not great but it gets you to the top of the formation. Awkward and grainy 5.9 move to 3rd class. After the first pitch, you can climb a diagonaling 5.6 pitch left to a tree, then rappel down and set a toprope on The Man Who Fell to Earth. Just to the left of Pony Express is a five-bolt 5.11b face variation called Under the Spreading Atrophy. This climb is usually toproped.

K. Only the Young Die Brave   5.11c★★

FA: Dave Kennedy, Will Chen, Mark Robinson, 1989.

Sustained 5.10 arête move to a baffling 5.12 crux. Toproping this and The Man Who Fell to Earth is a little involved; walk uphill 100 feet, then turn right and climb a 5.5 chimney. Once on top of the chimney, rappel from a tree to bolt anchors.

L. The Man Who Fell to Earth   5.11b★★★

FA: Paul Crawford, Dan Osman.

A few reachy and balancy 5.11 moves, then great 5.10 knob climbing to the top. Use a directional on the last bolt if toproping.

Short Topropes (not shown)

Right of Hyperspace, you can chimney up 20 feet of unprotected 5.7 chimney and set up a Toprope off bolts. On climbers' left there is a 5.10a and to the right is a 5.12a.

M. Hyperspace   5.10b★★★★

FA: Richard Harrison, Jay Smith, 1977.

Continuous underclinging on a fragile flake. Set a toprope by climbing to the fourth bolt of Unknown 5.10c and walking right on the ledge. The second pitch is runout and a little dirty on 5.7 knobby face. This pitch is rarely climbed.

N. Happy Face   5.10c★★★

FA: Aidan Maguire, Jerry Klatt, 2001.

A few 5.10 cruxes between easier face moves. Well-protected once you clip the first bolt (bring a few small nuts for the first 10 feet).

Northern Lights (not shown)   5.12a★★

FA: Scott Bye.

Located about 50 feet left of Happy Face. Dirty, easy climbing to steep 5.12a dihedral. Bring long slings for anchor.
Rack: cams: 2 ea .5-2"

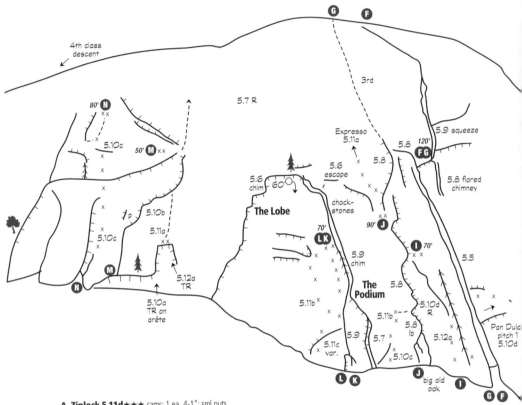

A. **Ziplock 5.11d**★★★ cams: 1 ea .4-1"; sml nuts

B. **The Ghost in the Machine 5.12a**★★★★ cams: 1 ea .4-3"; RPs

C. **Sugar Daddy 5.11c**★★★★

D. **Fat Merchant's Crack 5.10a X**★★★ cams: 1 ea 5-9"

E. **Grand Delusion 5.12d**★★★★ nuts: 1 ea .4-1"

F. **TM's Deviation 5.10a**★★★★ cams: 1-2 ea .5-1", 2 ea 1.25-5"

G. **West Chimney 5.8**★★ cams: 1-2 ea .5-3.5"

H. **Expresso 5.11a**★★★ draws

I. **Cry Uncle 5.12a R**★★★ cams: 1 ea .4-1", RPs, 3 draws

J. **Pony Express 5.8**★★★★ cams: 1 ea .5-3.5"

K. **Only the Young Die Brave 5.11c**★★ cams: 1 ea 1-4" (optional); 5 draws

L. **The Man Who Fell to Earth 5.11b**★★★ 6 draws; optional 1" piece

M. **Hyperspace 5.10b**★★★★ cams: 2 ea .4-2"

N. **Happy Face 5.10c**★★★ cams: 1 ea .4-.6"; 7 draws

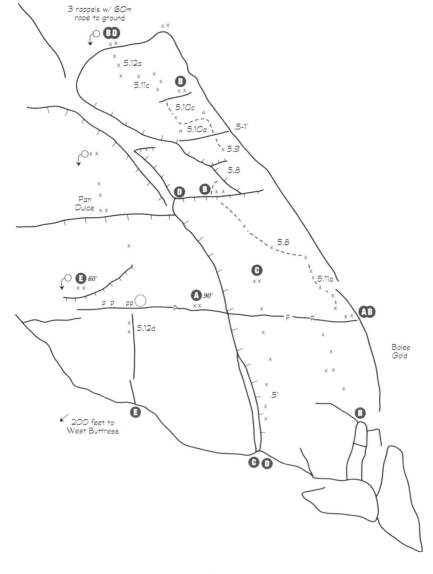

West Buttress

Approach time: **25 minutes**

Sun exposure: **noon to sunset**

Height of routes: **100'**

This is one of the easier crags on which to establish a toprope. It offers a high concentration of low-angle face climbs in the 5.7 to 5.10 range. Most routes have a bouldery start that feels harder than the route's rating and then finish on easier terrain. The rock is more flakey than other areas at Sugarloaf. Half of the climbs are completely bolted and half are mostly bolted but require some gear. All routes are put up by Jerry Klatt and Ron Brown. Jerry deserves recognition for the many hours of thankless work building and repairing trails, meeting and writing letters to local officials and land owners, making notice boards, and installing food boxes at Lover's Leap.

Chris McNamara

A. Sciatica 5.10d★★ draws
B. Cryptogamic 5.7★★ nuts, cams: 1-2 ea .5-2.5"
C. Scratchin' It 5.9★ draws
D. Knobelty 5.10b★★ draws
E. Pickin' It 5.9★ draws
F. The Left Cheek 5.8★★ draws
G. Sacroiliac Joint 5.7★★ nuts, cams: 1-2 ea .5-3.5"
H. Long Toe 5.8★★ draws
I. Middle Toe 5.9★★ draws
J. Short Toe 5.10b★★ draws

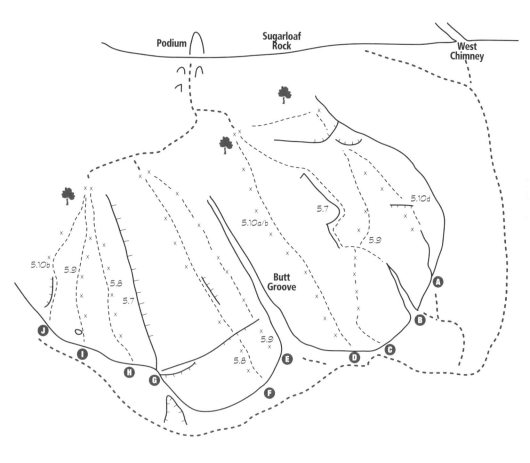

Phantom Spires

The Phantom Spires were so named because they were once hidden in a dense forest. Then a fire incinerated the hillside, clearing a view to The Spires and so today the name doesn't make much sense. The network of 15 to 20 spires starts just above Highway 50 and stretches 800 vertical feet up a wind-swept ridge. They are clearly visible and possess warm tones of gold and white granite that invite you to climb them.

The high-quality granite is covered with dikes, large knobs, roofs, and clean corners. Many faces are splashed with orange, brown, and black as if they just popped out of the toaster. The climbs are steep and the knobs are generally huge, positive, and spaced out (it's good to be tall).

Half the climbs are cracks and half are well bolted (there are few runouts). Many routes also have optional or mandatory knob-tieoffs. Most anchors are bolted with chains that make the climbing convenient and conducive to getting a lot of pitches in a day.

History

The Phantom Spires that climbers enjoy today is completely different from The Spires of years ago. Today it's a prominent feature, easily located. Not so on my first visit in April of 1975. My main climbing partner, Rob Oravetz, had been taken by members of our Hoot Owl Mountaineer climbing club to this little known and mysterious spot a few days earlier. Because of rainy weather they hadn't done any serious climbing, but what Robert saw impressed him to the point that he recruited me to attempt his "dream route." With wild-eyed enthusiasm he described a beautiful, knob-covered wall leading to a good ledge. "Then," he continued, "a hideous looking offwidth shoots to the top, and that can be your lead!" Not knowing what to expect, I agreed and soon found myself humping up the arduous approach through a dense pine forest from Highway 50. As we hiked up the steep forested ridge, I could not help but be impressed with the weird and fantastic formations we passed. It became clear why the area had been named "Phantom Spires." Finally, as the Upper Spire came into view, Robert pointed out his intended route. It was much larger and steeper than I had imagined. Thus, "Jugs Revisited" was conceived and climbed by a pair of relatively inexperienced climbers. On the same day Robert also led the long thin crack on the left side of the same face, what became "Robert's Crack." I recall that this direct aid ascent used up a lot of pitons.

For a few years we Hoot Owls had Phantom Spires pretty much to ourselves. Along with Rob and myself, other Hoot Owls active during this period were Dave Babich, Dan Chan, Dave Croy, Don and Rich Spittler, and Kevin Rivett. Then, with the appearance of the rival Ghoulwe Mountaineering Club, the ante was upped. Both groups started working on more difficult lines and aid eliminations. Some of the notable Ghoulwe climbers during that period were Eric Barrett, John Bowlin, Dave Stam, and Mark Hudon. The competition for routes was both serious and good-natured. We collaborated on many first ascents, one of the more notable ones being Candyland. Rob Oravetz handled the bold lead with Ghoulwes Eric Barrett and Jon Bowlin following.

There were also sporadic visits by other groups of climbers. The first ascents of the two fine dihedrals, "Fear of Flying" and "Lean and Mean," were done by the teams of Sierra Club climbers Joel Moore and Dale Zgraggen and Joel Moore and Bob Grow, respectively.

Prior to our activity at Phantom Spires, some climbing had been done, but had not been well documented. The contents of an old metal film canister found in the initial finger crack of the Regular Route on Lower Spire gave first ascent information for that climb and was signed by Roger Moreau and Russ Hoopes, with a date of 1955! We had also heard rumors that the late Warren Harding had visited the area and assumed that the few rusted old ringed angle pitons we found were his. At one point Dan Chan called Warren at his home in West Sacramento to ask for information on the climbs he had done at The Spires. Warren said that so much time had elapsed that he could not remember any specifics. He did remember that he had done "some climbs up there" and recalled a chimney he had done with John Ohrenshall. We did indeed find a rusty ringed angle piton fixed in a flake crack at the start of a climb we took the liberty to name "Harding's Other Chimney." This is the obvious chimney to the left of Candyland on Middle Spire that has been mistakenly located on Ham & Eggs Buttress in previous guidebooks.

Those were the old days: climbing in a place both outstanding and hard to find. Then came the fire in the early 1980s that changed everything. When I visited the area immediately after the fire the actual damage seemed spotty. But somebody decided to clear-cut the area. To me it seemed uncalled for, but hey, what do I know? The entire ridge was now open to full view and new route activity began in earnest by stronger South Lake Tahoe climbers such as Jay Smith and Paul Crawford. Needless to say, with most of the obvious natural lines already climbed, attention was focused on the blank faces. Wild, bolt-protected face climbs began to sprout up. Personally, it is somewhat disheartening to see such a profusion of bolts on almost every formation. Many of the little 25 to 30-foot walls we toproped for practice are now bolted as lead climbs. In some cases bolts have been added to climbs that had been led free on natural protection. But what can I say? This area belongs to all climbers. We had our day in the sun.

– George Connor

Toproping Beta

Climb one route and you can usually toprope a few others from the same anchor with one 60m rope. Leading 5.8 gets you on top of most Spires from where you can set topropes on harder climbs. However, to sample all The Spires have to offer, ideally you should lead 5.9 or harder and toprope 5.10 or harder. The only cliffs you can walk or scramble to the top to set toprope anchors are: The Blocks, East Face of Lower Spire, Clam Rock, Right Side of Phantom Wall, Left Side of Twin Owls.

Getting There

If traveling east from San Francisco on Highway 50: About 30 minutes past Placerville you pass through the tiny town of Kyburz. Continue east on Highway 50 for 4.9 miles and take a left on Wrights Lake Road.

If traveling west from South Lake Tahoe on Highway 50: About 25 minutes past South Lake Tahoe you pass through Strawberry and Lover's Leap. Continue west on Highway 50 for 4.2 miles and turn right onto Wrights Lake Road.

On Wrights Lake Road, drive 2.2 miles and turn left onto a dirt logging road (from here you get a great view of Phantom Spires). On the logging road it's about a half mile to the parking area. NOTE: The first 100 yards of the logging road are rocky; low-clearance cars may hit bottom. If you love your low-clearance car, park on Wrights Lake Road and walk the logging road (this adds 15 minutes to the approach).

Approach

From the end of the logging road, walk a climbers' trail west. After five minutes, you reach the Middle Spire and a variety of trails leading to the surrounding Spires. The closest climbs take about three minutes to get to and the farthest Spires take 15 minutes to get to.

GPS Coordinates

Wrights Lake Road turnoff of Highway 50:
38º 47' 422", 120º 13' 930"
Turnoff for logging road:
38º 47' 422", 120º 13' 933"
First Campground major pullout:
38º 47' 563", 120º 14' 210"
Parking Area:
38º 47' 400", 120º 14' 511"
Rock below Twin Owls:
38º 47' 319", 120º 14' 527"
Lost John:
38º 47' 365", 120º 14' 789"

When to Climb

Phantom Spires can have great weather year-round but the best times to climb are February-May and September-November. Luckily The Spires face all directions and moving from sun to shade or escaping the wind involves walking fewer than a hundred feet.

The fire opened up great views of the surrounding mountains and the other spires. However, with no trees to buffer the wind, there's a constant breeze that often builds to a disruptive gale. If high winds are forecast for either Kyburz or Twin Bridges, climb instead at either Lover's Leap or Sugarloaf. Generally the higher elevation Spires have more wind. Some of the more wind sheltered cliffs: The Blocks; Twin Owls; Middle Spire; East Face; Lower Spire; Southeast Face; Phantom Wall; Gorilla Rock.

For a weather forecast, check both Kyburz and Twin Bridges at:
www.weather.com/weather/local/USCA0559
www.weather.com/weather/local/USCA1174

March–May

When there is no snow on Wrights Lake Road, it's usually ok to climb at The Spires. In March expect few crowds but icy temperatures if the wind kicks up. By April The Spires are usually in prime condition with temperatures in the 50-60s. Monitor the weather closely as icy winds and snow can be expected at least a week out of each month.

June–August

In June the temperatures heat up and it's time to seek the shade of the north-facing climbs. July and August are usually too hot to climb and it's better to go climb at Lover's Leap or Wrights Lake. Storms are rare.

September–November

September usually has a few Indian summer weeks before cooling down to pleasant conditions. October is usually perfect. November has a few weeks of great weather before the first winter storms arrive.

December–February

Climb all winter in a low snow year. However, just a slight breeze can make the climbs uncomfortably cold so monitor the weather closely. Snowy roads are another concern; the logging road usually holds snow from December through March. Park on Wrights Lake Road and walk the snowy logging road; this only adds 15 minutes to the approach. However, if Wrights Lake Road has snow (it's not plowed) then there is probably more snow at Phantom Spires than you want to deal with. Go to Sugarloaf.

Camping

Camping is conveniently located at the Phantom Spires parking lot, along the logging road, and along Wrights Lake Road. It's all Forest Service land so you can camp just about anywhere. There are three large pullouts along the logging road that each accommodate 4 to 8 cars. The first two have nice views but are often windy. The last pullout, the Phantom Spires parking area, is the largest and most wind-sheltered. There is also a great camping spot at the end of a 4WD road that leads to just below Lizard Head. There are no facilities so bring your own water and bury your poop at least 6 inches underground. Be careful when building a fire. Build a tall fire-ring and keep fires small, especially when it's windy. Fire permits are required for fires and are available at the ranger station at 7887 Highway 50, Pollock Pines; 530-644-2349.

Cell Phones

You get a strong cell signal on top of spires, ridges, and at certain points on Wrights Lake Road. In most other areas, including the campsites, there is no cell signal.

Rescue

In case of injury there is a rescue litter bolted to rock a few hundred feet east of the Middle Spire. However, if you suspect a spinal injury it's best to call 911 and let emergency rescue workers transport the injured climber.

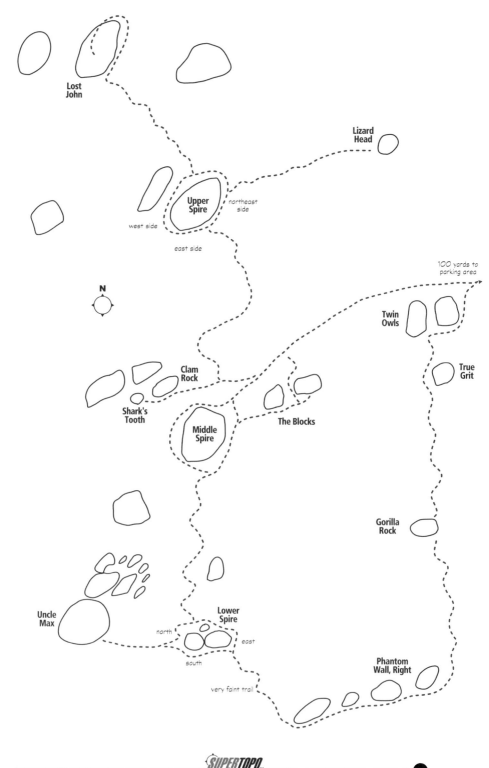

Lost
John

Lizard
Head

Upper
Spire

northeast
side

west side

east side

100 yards to
parking area

N

Twin
Owls

True
Grit

Clam
Rock

Shark's
Tooth

Middle
Spire

The Blocks

Gorilla
Rock

Uncle
Max

Lower
Spire

north

east

south

Phantom
Wall, Right

very faint trail

Lizard Head

Approach time: **20 minutes**

Sun exposure: **partial all day**

Height of routes: **25–40'**

Lizard Head makes up for its small size with striking symmetry and inviting white rock. Few climbers visit this rock because of the difficult climbing and deceptively long approach. While you can drive within a few hundred feet of the rock, dense brush mandates an a circuitous approach of walking to the Upper Spire then back east to Lizard Head.

A. Lounge Lizard 5.10c★★★★

FA: Mike Kreal, Larry Von Wald, 9/01.

Well-protected face climbing over small roofs. Optional small cams in horizontal crack after the third bolt. The easiest way to reach the summit and toprope other climbs. To the left is a 5.10d toprope.

Rack: cams: 1 ea .6-1"; 6 draws

B. South Face A3★★

Horizontal cracks and vertical seems. Good aid practice.

C. Dewlap 5.11d★★★

FA: John Scott, Troy Croliss, 8/90.

Vertical to overhanging edge-pulling from the west arête to the north arête.

Rack: 6 draws

North Face (not shown) 5.11c★★

FA: Jay Smith, 1986.

Fun toprope left of Dewlap. Move more left to toprope the East Arête (5.10a A1).

opposite: Antonio Carrion on Dewlap (5.11d). (Jim Thornburg)

Lost John

Approach time: **15 minutes**

Sun exposure: **partial all day**

Height of routes: **110'**

Chris McNamara

Unlike the surrounding free-standing spires, Lost John rises out of the hillside like the bow of a sunken ship. The longer approach and more challenging climbs result in few crowds. Descend by scrambling (some 4th class) to the north side.

A. Unknown   5.12a★★

Short and well-bolted.
Rack: 3 draws

B. Scrubby's Crossing   5.12c★★★★★

FA: Jeff Follet.

Crux features an insecure lieback in a cool shallow corner above third bolt. Sustained and funky jams and face holds to the anchor. Place some gear before the first bolt.
Rack: cams: 1 ea .5-1", 8 draws

C. Whole Slot of Trouble   5.11d★★★

FA: Jay Smith, 1991.

Climb a deceivingly hard crack on the salient orange prow. The bolt-protected crux climbs an awkward, polished flared crack.
Rack: cams: 2 ea .4-3"

D. Turning Point   5.10b★★★

FA: Don Spittler, David Babich, 1976.
FFA: Eric Barrett, George Connor, 1978.

One of the better 5.10 cracks at Phantom Spires. Well-protected with rests between a couple of steep 5.10 stemming cruxes and a short awkward flare. Steeper than it looks. One bolt and 1-1.5" cams for anchor. Nice step up in difficulty after Fear of Flying. First ascensionist Eric Barrett felt this climb signaled a turning point in difficulty standards at Phantom Spires.
Rack: cams: 2 ea .6-2.5", 1 ea 3.5"

Unnamed (not shown)   5.8★

From Turning Point, walk 80 feet up and left to the west face and look for bolts. This 60-foot route has sustained 5.7 and 5.8 face moves on somewhat flaky and dirty rock. There are two bolts low and two bolts high with a few horizontal cracks in the middle for gear. An okay first 5.8 lead or easy toprope by walking to the anchors. You can toprope other easier (but dirtier) routes from the same anchors. Descend by rappelling or walking off the north side.

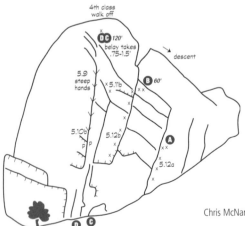

Chris McNamara pulls through the crux of Char Broiled (5.10d), Upper Spire.
(Sarah Felchlin)

Upper Spire

Approach time: 10 minutes

Sun exposure: partial all day

Height of routes: 90–200'

This is the tallest and most aesthetic spire with the highest concentration of four and five star climbs. Most routes are 5.9 or harder but all routes can be toproped after climbing either a 5.6 or 5.7 route. Descend most routes with one rappel down the northwest side from either the summit anchors or Harrison Direct (a great 5.11b toprope) or make two rappels down the south face with one 60m rope (convenient to toprope 5.11b Lesbian Love).

NORTHEAST SIDE

A. Desperado Roof Var. 5.10b★★

FA: David Babich, George Connor, 1978.

Climb the East Face Route, then move through the steep hand crack and wide-hand crack over the roof. The moves are powerful and well-protected.

B. East Face Route 5.9★

FA: George Connor, Dan Chan, 1976.

A serious lead. Broken flaky rock leads to a wide crack crux through a roof. Tunnel into the wide crack, place a medium nut, then exit the wide crack and climb runout face. George Connor named it East Face in the old Yosemite tradition to give the climb "more class." But for most routes, Connor and others followed modern naming convention in which climbs are named after popular songs, striking rock characteristics, a notable first ascent story, or the most common naming convention: something that just sounds cool.

C. Steppin' Stone 5.11a★★★★

FA: Eric Barrett, George Connor, Dave Stam, 1978.
FFA: Dick Richardson and friends, 1979.

A mixture of pumpy and technical climbing. Thought-provoking stemming crux leads to a big rest before a pumpy undercling/roof (have .6-.75" cams ready).

Chris McNamara

Difficult to toprope. The awesome second pitch has well-protected and sustained thin face moves between knobs. Occasional gear placements between bolts. Rappel the route or climb 40 feet of runout 5.6 face to the summit. From the first anchor it's easy to toprope Burnt Offerings and Holy Smoke.

D. Burnt Offerings 5.10d★★★

FA: Paul Crawford, Don Garret, 1982.

Thin moves and thin gear lead to a bolt and then an undercling out a roof to the left. Scary lead.

E. Holy Smoke 5.11c★★★★

FA: Aidan Maguire, 2000.

Sustained, balancy, and powerful climbing. Crux move at the fourth bolt is hard on the left shoulder. Optional gear under roof between the fourth and fifth bolts.

F. Unknown 5.11a★★★★

FA: unknown

After crossing Necklace Traverse, ascend face past a pin and a small roof. At the second roof move left onto the wildly exposed and gently overhanging arête. Climb the crack on it's left side for 20 feet before pulling back onto the right face.

Continue past one bolt up to the belay. This is an amazing and rarely done route. A trad classic in the true tradition.

G. Necklace Traverse   5.10d★★★★

FA: George Connor, D. Chan, 1977.
FFA: George Connor, Robert Oravetz, 1979.

Steep and exhilarating. Climb the first pitch of Fear of Flying. From the belay make a wild hand traverse right and meet ramp with thin protection to the second belay of Steppin' Stone. For the equally airy and more direct Hudon Variation, start up Fear of Flying and belay under a roof. Next, ascend the powerful crux bulge that you lieback and stem to the right leaning ramp. Beware of ropedrag if climbing in one pitch.

A. Desperado Roof Var. 5.10b★★ cams: 2 ea .6-4"
B. East Face Route 5.9★ cams: 2 ea .6-4.5" (optional 7-10")
C. Steppin' Stone 5.11a★★★★ cams: 2 ea .6-3"
D. Burnt Offerings 5.10d★★★ cams: 1 ea .5-1"
E. Holy Smoke 5.11c★★★★ cams: 1 ea .6-1"; 6 draws
F. Unknown 5.11a★★★★ cams: 1-2 ea .5-3.5"
G. Necklace Traverse 5.10d★★★★ cams: 2 ea .4-2"

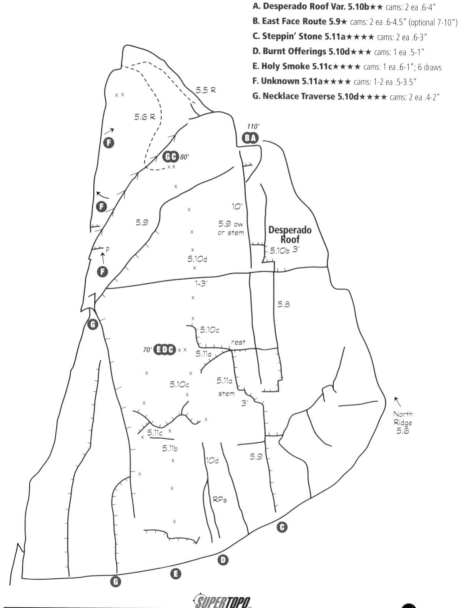

EAST SIDE

H. Fear of Flying   5.9★★★★★

FA: Joel Moorem, Dale Zgraggen, 1975.

One of the hardest and definitely the most classic 5.9 at Phantom Spires. Well-protected steep jamming mixed with delicate stemming and face. Beware of ropedrag if climbing in one pitch. Mark Hudon got attention when on his first visit to Phantom Spires in the mid-1970s, he onsight soloed the climb.

I. Gingerbread   5.7★★★★

FA: George Connor, Robert Oravetz, 1975.

A great introduction to Phantom Spires. Featured rock with a number of flakes to lieback, stem, or jam. The second pitch climbs the face left of a wide crack. Occasionally reach back in and place 2-4" cams for protection. Belay on a ledge after 150 feet or go all the way to the top in one 60m pitch. The featured rock with knobs, horns, and golden patina reminded the first ascensionists of gingerbread architecture—a style defined by gaudy ornamentation.

J. Jugs Revisited   5.9★★★★

FA: George Connor, Robert Oravetz, 1975.

After a brief 5.9 lieback crux, the route eases to sustained and almost runout 5.8. Hunt for hidden gear placements and knob tie-offs. Bring a few 2-4" cams to protect the last wide crack but climb left of the crack on the knobby face. Climb in one long pitch or two.

K. Lesbian Love   5.11c★★★★

FA: Aidan Maguire, 2002.

An exceptional, sustained, and tenuous face climb following a beautiful dike. Well-bolted but most climbers toprope it with a 60m rope after climbing any of the other routes on the south face (the anchor is the rap route down the east face).

Chris McNamara

L. T-Bone   5.10d★★

FA: Paul Crawford, Jay Smith Lanny Johnson, Mard Hudon, 1984.

Pretty good, pretty runout, usually toproped. Three old and spaced bolts then either 1) go into Robert's Crack. 2) go straight up on scary 5.11 with knob tie-offs for protection 3) Traverse into Lesbian Love.

M. Robert's Crack   5.10d★★

FA: George Connor, Robert Oravetz, 1975.
FFA: Eric Barrett, John Bowlin, 1979.

Hard 5.10b face moves to scary detached flake (possible to protect but you probably shouldn't). Gain the main crack system, clip a piton, and climb nice fingers and face to the base of a shallow dihedral. In the dihedral, crack becomes thin 5.10d protected with a piton and micro nuts. Stem and jam up to the roof and traverse left up to a small ledge. Either belay here or continue up to the top on 5.8 wide crack and knobs. Also possible to finish on Golden Brown. For a safer alternative start, go up Golden Brown to the second bolt and traverse in above the scary death flake.

N. Golden Brown   5.11d★★★★

FA: Petch Pietrolungo, Blue Blocker, 9/02.

Two 5.11 cruxes low before the exhilarating deadpoint crux on the gently overhanging golden arête. Finish on Char Broiled (bring cams: 1 ea .2-3.5") or left on the dirty one-bolt 5.8 original finish. Look for knob tie-offs. Can toprope with 70m rope.

O. Char Broiled   5.10d★★★★

FA: Karl McConachie, Paul Crawford, 1984.

Steep pinches and jams lead to a hard and reachy bolt-protected face crux (spooky clip for shorter climbers). Heady but positive knob climbing leads to easier terrain (with one brief 5.10a lieback move). Can toprope with a 70m rope (bring long slings for the anchor).

H. Fear of Flying 5.9★★★★★ cams: 2 ea .6-2"
I. Gingerbread 5.7★★★★ cams: 2 ea .6-3.5"
J. Jugs Revisited 5.9★★★★ cams: 1-2 ea .5-4"
K. Lesbian Love 5.11c★★★★ 9 draws
L. T-Bone 5.10d★★★ cams: 2 ea .6-2"
M. Robert's Crack 5.10d★★★ cams: 1-2 ea .4-3"
N. Golden Brown 5.11d★★★★ 9 draws; slings
O. Char Broiled 5.10d★★★★ cams: 2 ea .6-3"

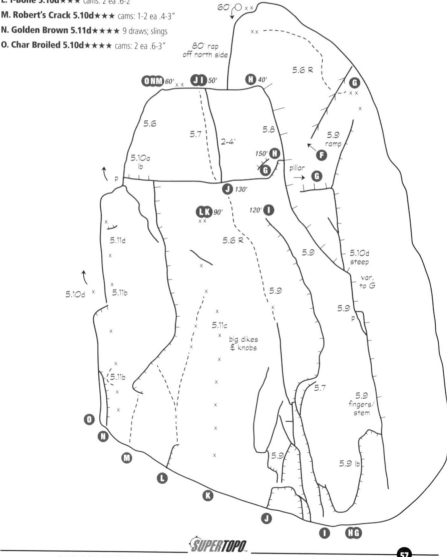

WEST SIDE

P. Well Done   5.11d★★

FA: Paul Crawford , Karl McConachie, 1984.

Flared crack that is harder than it looks.

Q. Crispy Critters   5.10a★

FA: Bill Price, Paul Crawford, Jay Smith, 1981.

Sustained liebacking up somewhat fragile and grainy flakes. Difficult to protect and rarely led.

R. Harrison Direct   5.11b★★★

FA: Aidan Maguire.

Usually toproped after climbing any of the routes on the south face. Climb a standard 5.10a lieback start or a 5.10a variation to the left. Up high, the 5.11b crux is steep, thin, and reachy. From the anchor, can toprope the first half of Crispy Critters.

S. Cabin Fever   5.11b/d★★★★

FA: Clint Cummins, Joel Ager, 3/90.

Uniquely carved rock with big knobs. Easy to toprope after climbing the North Ridge. 5.11d or harder if you are shorter than 5'9".

T. Sizzler   5.11b★★★★

FA: Jay Smith, Paul Crawford, 1986.

First pitch climbs a flared crack with tenuous jamming and tricky protection (this pitch only gets two stars). The second pitch has a unique mixture of steep crack and face in a stomach-turning position. Bold lead: usually toproped.

U. Up for Grabs   5.8★★★

FA: David Babich, Eric Barrett, 1978.

A fun start to North Ridge with big knobs and a few jams. Traverse left at roof/ horizontal crack.

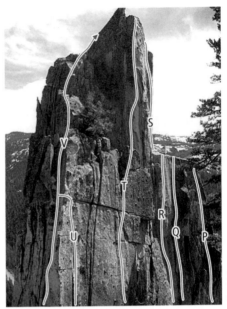

Chris McNamara

V. North Ridge   5.6★★★

FA: unknown

A great mini-alpine rock climb with moderate climbing and a cool summit. The crux is a steep but featured corner system off the ground followed by blocky 4th class climbing to a ridge traverse finale. Belay below the final ridge traverse on a big ledge. Shaded most of the day. Retreat by rappelling with one 60m rope down to the big ledge to the west and then rappel down Harrison Direct (if windy, manage the rope or it will snag).

P. Well Done 5.11d★★ cams: 2 ea .4-2"

Q. Crispy Critters 5.10a★ cams: 2 ea .6-3.5"

R. Harrison Direct 5.11b★★★ cams: 2 ea .5-1.5"

S. Cabin Fever 5.11b/d★★★★ 6 draws

T. Sizzler 5.11b★★★★ nuts: 1 set micro; cams: 1-2 ea .6-2"

U. Up for Grabs 5.8★★★ cams: 1-2 ea .6-4"

V. North Ridge 5.6★★★ cams: 1-2 ea .6-3"

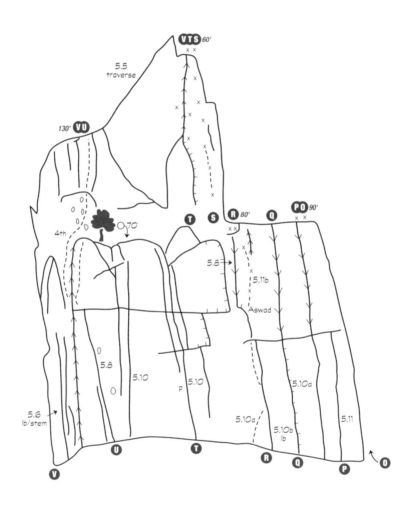

Shark's Tooth Clam Rock

Approach time: **5 minutes**

Sun exposure: **partial all day**

Height of routes: **25'**

The Shark's Tooth is small but has a cool summit. Its neighbor to the east, Clam Rock, hosts three bolted face routes. Each Clam Rock climb starts with a few desperate face moves before big knobs appear and the difficulties ease to 5.9 and 5.10 (many climbers pull on the first few bolts to get to the easier climbing). Scramble up 5.4 on the north side to toprope routes B and C. All routes require only quickdraws.

CLAM ROCK

A. Unnamed right route   5.12★★

Powerful start to fun featured rock. Bad toprope: anchor too far left.

B. Unnamed center route   5.10d★★★

Another thin and desperate start but at least there are some holds (unlike the climbs to the left and right).

C. Unnamed left route   5.12?★★

A seemingly impossible start (did a hold break?) leads to a featured arête. Toprope by using a directional on the last bolt.

SHARK'S TOOTH

D. 3-bolt Arête   5.10a★★★★

Excellent moves in a short space. Be careful clipping second bolt. (No topo, shown on photo.)

E. 1-bolt Arête   5.8★★★

Solo up 15 feet of 5.6, clip the bolt, and make a 5.8 move to the summit. Afterward, toprope the 5.10a arête.

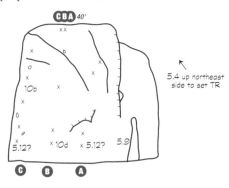

opposite: Sarah Felchlin pulling on the Shark's Tooth. (Chris McNamara)

Chris McNamara

Middle Spire

Approach time: 5 minutes

Sun exposure: partial all day

Height of routes: 60–130'

The most popular and accessible Phantom Spire. It has the most 5.7-5.8 routes as well as many quality 5.9 and 5.10 climbs. Toprope some climbs by walking to the anchors and toprope the others after leading Regular Route (5.8). Warm up in the morning sun on the wind-sheltered East Side. If not too windy, finish the day climbing in glowing evening light on the West Side.

Chris McNamara

NORTH SIDE

A. Slowdancer   5.9★★★

FA: Eric Barrett and friends, 1978.

An awkward and tricky-to-protect start leads to excellent knob climbing. The upper route protects with two bolts and knob tie-offs. Belay under the roof or move over to the Lean and Mean anchors. Or better yet, continue up Penny Candy to create one of the best link-ups at Phantom Spires.

B. Hard Up   5.9★★

FA: Eric Barrett, David Stam, 1977.

A short variation to Over Easy with a few fun 5.9 lieback moves. A good first 5.9.

C. Over Easy   5.7★★★★

FA: George Connor, Robert Oravetz.

The best 5.7 face climb at Phantom Spires. A thin bolt-protected 5.7 move leads to a cool 5.7 roof followed by big holds on a steep moderate wall. Protect with knob tie-offs and gear in horizontal cracks. Either belay under the roof on 1-3" cams or traverse left or right to bolt anchors. From the right bolt anchors, don't miss toproping Lean and Mean.

D. The Prow   5.10b★★★

FA: unknown

Well-bolted and exposed face climbing on good edges. A great finishing variation to Over Easy. To toprope, use long slings on the anchor. Don't miss the 5.10c toprope variation over the roof.

E. Cockabooty   5.7★★

FA: unknown

Three variations that get better from right to left. The right variation has mediocre rock and is a spooky lead.

EAST SIDE

F. Chainsaw Willie   5.8 R★★

FA: David Babich, 1982.

A mixture of friction, lieback, and steep face moves. The first and last crux have potential ledge falls. Use .6-1" cams to back up bolt in anchor. Rappel Regular Route to descend.

G. Tyro's Test Piece   5.5★★

FA: unknown

A great first introduction to Phantom Spires. Lieback down low and face climb up high. Set an anchor with .5-.1" cams and nuts (use a cordalete to equalize them). Walk off the ledge to descend.

H. Rain Song   5.7 R★★

FA: David Babich, 1980.

On this runout friction climb the bolt unfortunately comes after the first crux. After the bolt, climb straight up with no protection or move left to easier ground and a few gear placements.

I. Regular Route   5.8★★★

FA: unknown

A classic 5.8 crack that goes from hands, to wide hands, to lieback. Great for developing jamming technique. Most stop at the ledge and belay with a few 1-2" pieces rather than continue up the 5.8 chimney section. Confident 5.8 leaders might finish with Anal Sex. It's possible to walk to the anchor and set a toprope with one 50m or 60m rope.

J. Anal Sex   5.9 R★★

FA: Bill Serniuk, 5/88.

Hard lieback to runout 5.7 knobs. On the second pitch, climb a fun, featured, and runout face on mediocre gear. Can easily link both pitches.

A. Slowdancer 5.9★★★ cams: 1 ea .5-2"; 2 draws; slings
B. Hard Up 5.9★★ cams: 1 ea .4-2"; slings
C. Over Easy 5.7★★★★ cams: 1 ea .75-3.5"; slings for knob tie-offs
D. The Prow 5.10b★★★ 4 draws
E. Cockabooty 5.7★★ cams: 1-2 ea .4-2"
F. Chainsaw Willie 5.8 R★★ cams: 1 ea .6-2"
G. Tyro's Test Piece 5.5★★ cams: 1-2 ea .6-2"
H. Rain Song 5.7 R★★ cams: 1 ea .6-1.5"
I. Regular Route 5.8★★★ cams: 2 ea .75-3.5"
J. Anal Sex 5.9 R★★ cams: 1 ea .4-3.5"

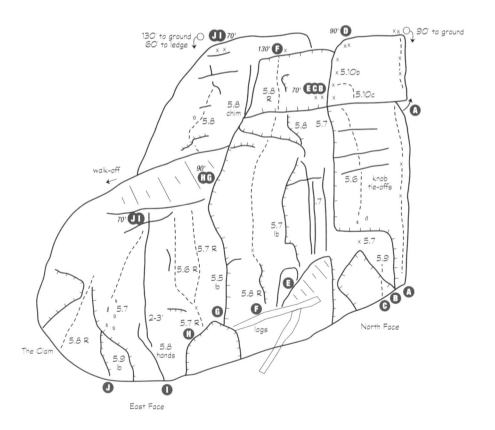

WEST SIDE

K. Candyland   5.10c★★★★★

FA: Eric Barrett, John Bowlin, Robert Oravetz, 1977.

One of the most memorable 5.10 pitches in Tahoe. Wild reaches between basketball-sized knobs on an overhanging wall. It's hard to tell what is more cool: the moves off the huge overhanging knobs or slinging the knobs as your only protection for most of the climb. The cruxes come between the second and third knob tie-offs and at the crack at end of the knobs. Even though the knobs offer solid protection, this is a spooky lead for some. To toprope the route, climb one of the easier routes on the east side.

Chris McNamara

L. Candy Ass   5.10d★★★

FA: Dave Hatchett, Tom Burt, 10/88.

A distinct knob pulling crux at the third bolt leads to sustained and tricky climbing on the arête. To toprope, use the Candyland anchor and clip a directional off the last bolt.

M. Harding's Other Chimney   5.7★★

FA: Warren Harding, John Ohrenschall, 1954.

A wide climbing adventure.

N. Unnamed   5.6★★

FA: unknown

A great first lead. Climb either left or right on featured rock, then make a 5.6 step up and left to the bolt anchor.

O. Fancy Dancin'   5.10b★★★

FA: Robert Oravetz, Eric Barrett, 1978.

Sustained thin crack with occasional knobs to short runout to a ledge with bolts. Stop at bolts or continue up steep knobs protected with tie-offs.

P. Corn Flakes   5.9★★★

FA: Robert Oravetz, Eric Barrett, Dave Stam, 1978.

Sustained liebacking on a thinning flake to a 5.9 face crux. At the crux go up the face or move right to an incipient seam. A little awkward to place protection and a little spooky at the top (look for the knob tie-off). Traverse left to Lean and Mean anchor. A runout 5.9 starting variation follows thin flakes to the right. Toprope this climb from the anchors of an unknown bolted route. Spot the two bolts (each with two metal links) from the ground, then gain the summit and get a belay while you reach over and clip the bolts.

Q. Lean and Mean   5.9★★★★

FA: Bob Grow, Joel Moore, 1976.

A sustained lieback and stemming corner with an insecure crux similar to Fear of Flying. This is a challenging 5.9 lead because the crux is difficult to protect and requires subtle body positioning. Most climbers stop at the anchors but there are three other options: 1) continue up Penny Candy 2) continue up the 5.6 chimney and set a toprope on Penny Candy 3) climb the 5.8 crack above the anchor, then pull through the bolts on an unnamed 5.12 to a two-bolt anchor and then toprope Corn Flakes.

R. Leaner and Meaner   5.11b★★★

FA: unknown

The testpiece Phantom Spires 5.11 finger crack. Start on Lean and Mean and move to the left crack when convenient. The crack thins from hands to powerful finger locks on steep wall. Easy to toprope after climbing Lean and Mean.

Penny Candy   5.10a★★★★

FA: Joel Ager, Clint Cummins, 8/90.

The recommended finish to Lean and Mean. Airy moves around a steep arête. Can toprope with one 60m rope.

Sarah Felchlin

Chris McNamara on the killer knob climb, Candyland.

K. Candyland 5.10c★★★★★ cams: 1 ea .4-1"; 4 slings
L. Candy Ass 5.10d★★★★ 7 draws
M. Harding's Other Chimney 5.7★★ cams: 1 ea .4-4"
N. Unnamed 5.6★★ cams: 1 ea .6-3"
O. Fancy Dancin' 5.10b★★★ cams: 1 ea .4-1.5"
P. Corn Flakes 5.9★★★ cams: 1-2 ea .6-2"
Q. Lean and Mean 5.9★★★★ cams: 2 ea .5-3"
R. Leaner and Meaner 5.11b★★★ cams: 2 ea .6-2"
Penny Candy 5.10a★★★★ 4 draws

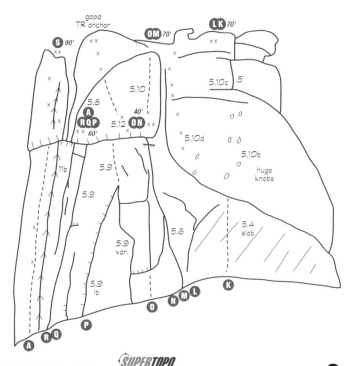

The Blocks

Approach time: 15 minutes

Sun exposure: morning to afternoon

Height of routes: 300'

The most accessible and wind-sheltered toproping area at Phantom Spires. The climbs are short but packed with steep quality moves. You can walk to the top of all anchors except Bowling Ball. All routes require 3-5 quickdraws.

A. The Bowling Ball   5.10b★★★

FA: Mike Kreal, Larry Von Wald, 4/89.

Big pulls between big knobs. Balancy finish. To reach the anchors and set a toprope, downclimb a short section of 5.5 (you probably want a belay).

B. Blue Note   5.10b★★

FA: Mike Kreal, Larry Von Wald, 4/89.

Small edges between big knobs and jugs.

C. French Letter   5.11a★★

FA: Mike Kreal, Larry Von Wald, 4/89.

One-move-wonder start followed by 5.10 reaches between knobs.

D. My Favorite Thing   5.10d★★

FA: Mike Kreal, Larry Von Wald, 4/89.

Powerful knob reach followed by cool arête climbing.

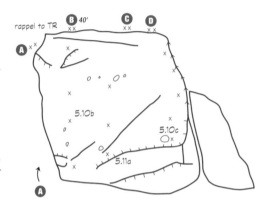

Chris McNamara

opposite: Mitch Underhill on The Bowling Ball. (Chris McNamara)

Twin Owls

Approach time: **2 minutes**

Sun exposure: **morning to afternoon**

Height of routes: **30–80'**

A few short but good topropes. Twin Owls offers the shortest approach at Phantom Spires and a few short and fun topropes. One of the more wind-sheltered and warmer spots. All routes require 3-4 quickdraws.

Chris McNamara

A. Unnamed Face/Crack   5.11a★★★

A mixture of thin crack and face. Well-protected at low cruxes. To set a toprope, scramble exposed fourth class to the right.

B. Unnamed   5.8★★★

Sustained 5.8 face moves on small but positive holds. Can set up toprope by scrambling up 4th class to the left.

C. Unnamed   5.8 TR★★★

Distinct knob crux low to sustained face moves. Can set up toprope by scrambling up 4th class to the left.

True Grit (not shown)

The next formation below Twin Owls. The crack on the west face starts at 5.10a and eases to 5.7 wide crack and knobs. On the south face is the Flying Wombat: a 5.11a with two bolts and #2 camalots for the belay. The rock around the anchor is a little rotten so back up your anchor with a long sling around something.

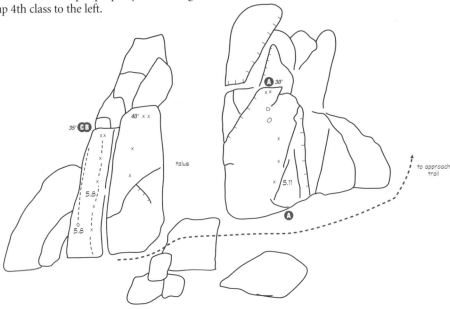

Gorilla Rock

Approach time: **12 minutes**

Sun exposure: **morning to afternoon**

Height of routes: **60'**

Gorilla Rock has three concentrated, sunny, and wind-sheltered 5.8 climbs. There is one two-bolt anchor to toprope the climbs and another two-bolt anchor for rappelling down the north side. Bring long slings for the anchor to reduce rope drag. Most climbers first lead Ko-Ko Box, then toprope the other two climbs. Another option is to climb the short and awkward 5.6 chimney section on the North Side. With only three climbs that share a single anchor, the crag is only suited for one group at a time.

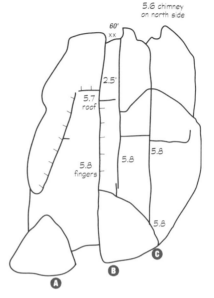

A. Ko-Ko Box   5.8★★★★

FA: Kevin Rivett, David Babich, 1977.

A quality 5.8 finger crack in a clean corner leads to a cool roof. Great first 5.8 trad lead.
Rack: cams: 1 ea .5-3.5"

B. Ant Crack, Left   5.8★★

FA: unknown

Face climb between the arête and thin crack. Worth a toprope after climbing Ko-Ko Box. A bold lead.
Rack: nuts: 1 set micro; cams: 1 ea .4-1"

C. Ant Crack, Right   5.8★★

FA: unknown

Face climbing around a thin crack. Usually toproped.
Rack: nuts: 1 set micro; cams: 1 ea .4-1"

Lower Spire

Approach time: **12 minutes**

Sun exposure: **late morning to afternoon**

Height of routes: **80–110'**

Lower Spire is not a single formation but two rocks separated by a chimney. It gets little traffic because the climbs are hard and spread out. The upper formation is the true spire and has a few excellent and challenging climbs that generally must be led. The lower formation has a 4th class scramble up the backside for establishing topropes. It's one of the few crags with trees, which buffer the wind.

Chris McNamara

NORTH SIDE

A. Five Tendons   5.10d★★

FA: Will Chen, 4/90.

Challenging crux right after the first bolt, then incredible large and steep edges to the anchor. Bring long slings to set toprope with 60m rope.

SOUTH SIDE

B. The Siren   5.11d★★

FA: Dave Rubine, Will Chen, 4/90.

One of the best 5.11 face climbs at Phantom Spires. Steep, sustained, and technical from bottom to top with a powerful roof crux high. Can toprope with 70m rope if you extend anchor with long slings. If you stop at the first anchor the climbs is 5.11a.

EAST SIDE

C. Last Lock-up   5.10c★★★★

FA: Dave and Mike Hatchett.

Fierce 5.9 jamming leads to sustained 5.10 liebacking then a roof crux. You can barely toprope it with a 60m rope if you extend the anchor 5 feet with slings.

D. Jack Corner   5.9★★★

FA: David Babich, D. Spittler, 1976.
FFA: Eric Barrett, Dave Stam, 1976.

Classic stemming corner with sharp fingerlocks. The uncommon crack shape requires thoughtful jams. Can barely toprope with 60m rope if you extend the anchor 5 feet with slings.

E. Fire Fly   5.5 R★★

FA: unknown

Fun knob climbing on decent quality rock. Most climbers set a toprope by scrambling up 4th class to the Jack Corner anchors. If leading, don't place gear until after the crux 30 feet up.

A. Five Tendons 5.10d★★ 6 draws
B. The Siren 5.11d★★★ 10 draws
C. Last Lock-up 5.10c★★★★ cams: 2 ea .6-2"; 3 draws
D. Jack Corner 5.9★★★ cams: 1 ea .6-3"
E. Fire Fly 5.5 R★★ cams: 1 ea .75-2.5"

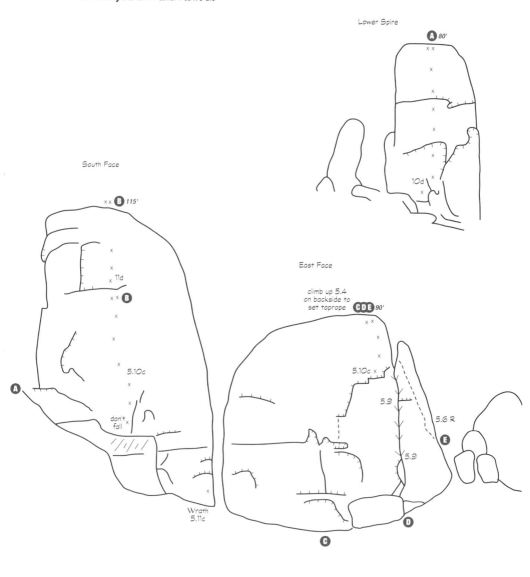

Lower Spire

Ⓐ 80'

South Face

B 115'

11d

Ⓑ

5.10c

don't fall

Ⓐ

Wrath
5.11c

East Face

climb up 5.4
on backside to
set toprope CDE 90'

5.10c

5.9

5.6 R

Ⓔ

5.9

Ⓓ

Ⓒ

10d

Phantom Wall, Right

Approach time: **20 minutes**

Sun exposure: **late morning to afternoon**

Height of routes: **80–110'**

Phantom Wall is a 100-yard-wide rock band composed of four individual rocks. We only include the right-most formation because the other rocks are lower-angle, more broken, and don't have a high concentration of good climbs. There is no clear approach trail to the climbs. From the Lower Spire work your way about 200 yards down and left until you are at the base of the rocks and then skirt the base to the major formation furthest east. You can also approach from Gorilla Rock by following a faint climbers' trail (see map).

It's a pain to reach the top of the climbs and establish topropes. You must walk left (west) to the first gully where you can get up without 5th class climbing then circle back around to the top. One of the most wind-sheltered areas.

A. Unnamed   5.12a★★★★

Fun lieback start that protects well with medium cams. Hand-traverse left out the flake then step right at the thin face crux. A few desperate moves lead to more moderate and airy arête finish. Tall climbers can pull through the crux using the bolt. Rappel to descend.

B. Oedipus Rex   5.7★★★

FA: Kevin Rivett, David Babich, 1975.

Climb the tree for 30 feet until then sink your hands into the sustained 5.7 hand and off-hands crack. Face climb around the brief wide section. Toprope with a 60m rope by extending the anchor 10 feet with slings.

Chris McNamara

C. Electra   5.11c★★★★

FA: Kevin Rivett, David Babich, 1977.
FFA: Dave and Mike Hatchett, 6/90.

A bouldery start with a bolt-protected, powerful undercling. Continue up the stellar 5.9 finger crack. To toprope with a 60m rope you need to extend the anchor 10 feet with long slings.

D. Dr. Jeckel and Mr. Hyde   5.11b★★★★

FA: Tom Smith, Krista Smith, Larry Von Wald, 1984.

Make well-protected face moves past three bolts and then move to the crack. Reachy crux between the second and third bolts.

E. Eraser Head   5.11b★★★

FA: David Babich, Kevin Rivett, 1980.

The climbing is a little runout on 5.8 and 5.7 but there is always a bolt near a 5.9 or 5.10 move.

A. Unnamed 5.12a★★ cams; 2 ea 1-3.5"; 8 draws

B. Oedipus Rex 5.7★★★ cams: 2 ea .75-4"

C. Electra 5.11c★★★★ cams: 1-2 ea .5-2.5"

D. Dr. Jeckel and Mr. Hyde 5.11b★★★★ cams: 2 ea .5-2.5"; 3 draws

E. Eraser Head 5.11b★★★ 7 draws

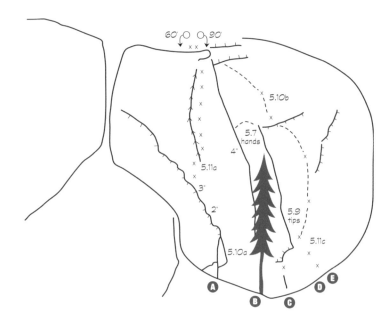

Wrights Lake

Wrights Lake has many single-pitch 5.10-5.12s in a secluded and pristine setting. The views are expansive and exceptional swimming holes sit just a few minutes away. There is an even mixture of mostly well-protected face climbs and crack routes on featured rock. Even non-climbers can appreciate this area as the main hangout area is a flat half-acre of granite with fine views and the ability to see all the climbs.

History

I've never been so reluctant to recommend an area. There's a side of me that worries about this pristine spot where I got married, put up routes, swam, and watched the mountains turn orange. I wonder if others will appreciate and care for it the way we have. I hope so. I hope they come equipped with strong fingers, delicate feet, and a cool head because the routes don't give much away.

This area got its start about 10,000 years ago when a kindly glacier carved it along with a set of perfect swimming holes. They say that Harding climbed out here back in the day, and the early developers found a couple of old pins as evidence. Bob Branscomb made reference to it in his tiny guide, *Crystal Basin Climbs*, but gave few details. In approximately 1986 Chris Craig, Mike Creel, and Steve Harvey from Davis got to work on many of the best lines, and around 1987 Troy Corliss and Larry VonWald joined them. This crew plus family and friends spent many weekends climbing here through 1991, and the results are many of the excellent lines seen today. The routes were a mixture of lead and rap bolts, and because of this and what they saw as an intolerant climate of bolt chopping, they made the conscious decision not to promote the area. In 1992 I began visiting the area with friends, but it was not till 1996 that I felt compelled to break out the wire brush and begin new route activity.

There are some truly excellent lines out here that will test your metal and your forearms, but climbing at Wrights Lake will always be more than just a day of pulling down. It's a day spent in a sublime area enjoying the best the mountains have to offer. Please handle it with care.

– Aidan Maguire

Toproping Beta

Most climbs are easy to toprope by walking to the top, leaning over the edge and clipping a two-bolt anchor. A 60m rope is mandatory for toproping many climbs, a few climbs require a 70m rope, and a few more require two ropes.

To reach the top and set a toprope:
A) Climb a route to the top of the cliff (the easiest one is The Prow (5.10a) or
B) Walk to either the far right or far left side of the cliff and scramble up to the top.

Getting There

If traveling east from San Francisco on Highway 50: About 30 minutes past Placerville you pass through the tiny town of Kyburz. Continue east on Highway 50 for 4.9 miles and take a left on Wrights Lake Road.

If traveling west from South Lake Tahoe on Highway 50: About 25 minutes past South Lake Tahoe you pass through Strawberry and Lover's Leap. Continue west on Highway 50 for 4.2 miles and turn right onto Wrights Lake Road.

On Wrights Lake Road, drive about 8 miles (takes about 20 minutes) to Wrights Lake and take the right fork around the lake to the Twin Lakes/Grouse Lake trailhead.

Approach

The approach takes about 30 minutes at a leisurely pace and 20 minutes if you are hoofing it. It is about 1.25 miles long with a very minimal change in elevation.

From the Northeast corner of the parking lot, hike the Twin Lakes/Grouse Lakes Trail for about a 0.5 miles until you merge with another trail. Walk another 50

Chris McNamara

yards east and look for a 25-foot-tall bluff 200 feet north of the trail. Skirt the right side of the bluff and the climbers' trail becomes obvious. Walk north for another 0.5 miles on climbers' trail and open slab until the cliff is on the right.

When to Climb

The climbing season is limited to when Wrights Lake Road is clear of snow. In a light snow year, the road may be open by early June. In a heavy snow year, however, the road does not open until the 4th of July. You can usually climb here until the first winter storm, sometime in November.

The west-facing walls are shaded until 11 a.m. and the north-facing walls are in the shade until 2 p.m. Once out of the shade, the climbs get intense direct sun until sunset. Climb here on summer mornings or spring and fall afternoons. As a general rule, if it's warmer than 90 degrees in Sacramento, then you don't want to climb in the sun.

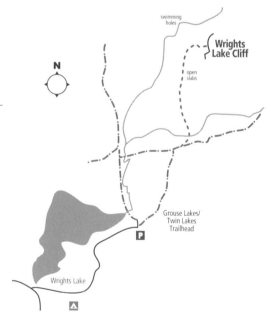

Wrights Lake

Approach time: **30 minutes**

Sun exposure: **late morning to afternoon**

Height of routes: **80–130′**

Chris McNamara

MAIN WALL

NOTE: There are another dozen or so topropes and bolted climbs to the left of Ah NUTTS.

A. Ah NUTTS   **5.13a★★★★**

FA: Troy Corliss, 1991.

Sixty feet of steep and powerful jams and liebacking. Three bolts, then smaller cams. You can toprope by rapping down from The Prow.

B. The Prow   **5.10a★★★★★**

FA: Chris Craig, late 1980s.

Great warm-up for the area. Start with slab climbing to a bushy ledge. Next, steeper and more sustained gear-protected moves. Be aware of rope drag. A .5" cam protects moves to the first bolt on headwall.

C. The Infinite   **5.10d★★★★**

FA: Aidan Maguire, 2003.

Tenuous stemming and chimney in an intimidating corner. Move right after corner onto arête. 5.10b bulge finish. Great nut placements.

D. The Fin   **5.11c or 5.10b A0★★★★**

FA: Steve Harvey, Chris Craig, late 1980s.

Face climbing in a great position on a huge fin of rock. The one-move crux is easily aided through to make the route 5.10b A0.

E. Spud Crack   **5.10c★★★★**

There are two options on this climb:
1) Follow the main dihedral up and left on slightly dirty 5.10c and finish on The Fin.
2) Pull over the big scary block on 5.10d moves and continue to the Black Stain anchor.

F. Oil Slick   **5.11d★★★★★**

FA: Steve Harvey.

Sustained face moves on cool knobs that gets better quality the higher you climb. The scary clip at the third bolt has resulted in one broken ankle. To make this move safe, rappel in and clip a long sling to the bolt. After third bolt is the crux moving left, then move back right.

G. Triple Bat Crack   **5.10d★★**

Fun 5.8 climbing to a 5.10d crux move then 5.10a to the top.

H. Slopey Saucers   **5.11b★★**

High-quality technical sloping knobs on a well-protected face.

I. Fish Supper   **5.10a★★**

FA: Aidan Maguire.

Crux is at the bottom but upper part is harder than it looks.

A. Ah NUTTS 5.13a ★★★★ cams: 2 ea .4-1.5"; 3 draws
B. The Prow 5.10a ★★★★★ cams: 2 ea .4-2.5"
C. The Infinite 5.10d ★★★ cams: 1-2 ea .4-2"
D. The Fin 5.11c or 5.10b A0 ★★★★ cams: 1 ea .4-1", 7 draws
E. Spud Crack 5.10c ★★★★ cams: 1-2 ea .4-2"

F. Oil Slick 5.11d ★★★★★ 9 draws
G. Triple Bat Crack 5.10d ★★★ cams: 1-2 ea .4-2"
H. Slopey Saucers 5.11b ★★★
I. Fish Supper 5.10a ★★★ cams: 1-2 ea .5-2"

SPECTRUM TOWER

J. Ultraviolet   5.11b★★★★

FA: Aidan Maguire.

There are three starts: 5.8 crack left of the
offwidth, the offwidth, or climb up the
ledge to the top of Fish Supper. For the
"Indigo" variation, start on Infrared and at
the third bolt traverse left into Ultraviolet.

K. Infrared   5.12a★★★★★

FA: Aidan Maguire.

Bouldery start or 5.0 traverse in from the
right to first bolt. Must backclip first bolt
after clipping second bolt. Optional gear
(but must remove after clipping bolt) to
sustained face and a devious crux move
right to the arête. Rest under the roof and
then finish on the 5.11b fingers crux of
Ultraviolet.

L. Spanish Flamethrower   5.11c★★★★

FA: Mike Creel.

Technical face on the arête with a very
insecure clip.

M. Avoidance   5.10b★★

FA: Aidan Maguire.

Crack right of arête.

Acrobat (not shown)   5.12a★★★★★

FA: Troy Corliss, 1991.

Cool sport route on the tower across the
brush-filled gully to the right of the Black
Beauty Wall. Twenty feet above the ledge
there is a 20-foot section of sustained
climbing. Pumpy roofs on big jugs to
technical finishing moves. Bolts and one
optional sml/med cam half way up.

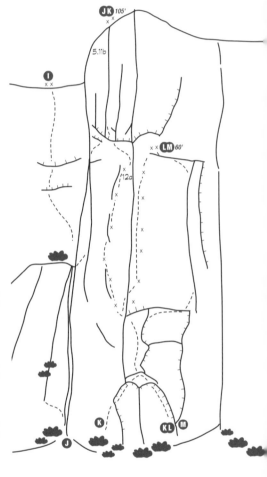

J. Ultraviolet 5.11b★★★★ cams: 2 ea .4-2"
K. Infrared 5.12a★★★★★ cams: 1 ea .4-1"; 7 draws
L. Spanish Flamethrower 5.11c★★★★ 7 draws
M. Avoidance 5.10b★★ cams: 1-2 ea .4-2.5"

BLACK BEAUTY WALL

For a killer crack workout, lead Velvet Gloves, then traverse on 5.6 moves to the anchors of Spanish Inquisition and Essence. With one carefully placed rope, you can toprope all three climbs. You can also establish topropes by rapping in from an anchor at the top of the wall.

Chris McNamara

N. Triple Decker   5.11b★★★

FA: Aidan Maguire.

Better than it looks. Blind nut placement above first bolt. Work up and left into short left-facing dihedral and finish on overhanging crack to anchor.

O. Spanish Inquisition   5.12b★★★★

FA: Aidan Maguire.

Superb and sustained hard crack climbing with bouldery crux lunge at the second bolt.

P. Essence   5.11d★★★★★

FA: Aidan Maguire.

Brilliant and super sustained. Crux lieback section at about 25 feet.

Q. Velvet Gloves   5.10b★★★★

FA: Aidan Maguire.

Great flared finger crack.

R. Lusty Vicar   5.10d★★

FA: Aidan Maguire.

Fun crack with tight hands crux pulling the roof at top.

S. Unknown   5.11c★★★

Fun sport climb. Optional piece below first bolt.

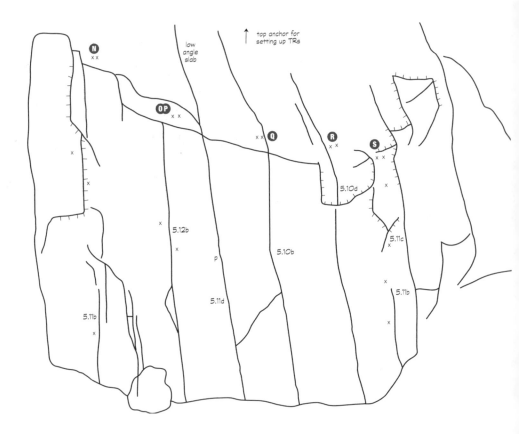

N. **Triple Decker 5.11b**★★★ cams: 1-2 ea .4-2"

O. **Spanish Inquisition 5.12b**★★★★ cams: 2 ea .4-1", 1 ea 1.25-2"

P. **Essense 5.11d**★★★★★ many sml nuts; cams: 2 ea .4-1", 1 ea 1.25-2"

Q. **Velvet Gloves 5.10b**★★★★ cams: 1-2 ea .6-2.5"

R. **Lusty Vicar 5.10d**★★★ cams: 2 ea .5-2"

S. **Unknown 5.11c**★★★ 7 draws

Lover's Leap

Lover's Leap boasts some of the country's best moderate granite. According to Royal Robbins in his 1976 Tahoe Guide, "With the lone exception of Tahquitz Rock, Lover's Leap has the best selection of concentrated free climbs in California... No one cliff even in Yosemite has Lover's Leap's concentration... with such quality and variety." Yosemite Valley offers better long routes, scenery, and history, but Lover's Leap has more easy and moderate multi-pitch climbs.

What makes Lover's Leap unique are the criss-crossed dikes, which form juggy meridians at 3 to 10 foot intervals. The dikes form when intrusive rock weathers more slowly than the surrounding granite. The myriad rock features offer many options for each crux which can help or confuse. The easiest climbing may be improbable face moves to the side of a major crack. Some 5.8 moves, the crux on Haystack for example, feel like 5.7 with perfect beta or 5.10 if you miss a key hold. The features also mean that it's a good idea to place slings on most pieces to reduce rope drag.

Crucial Leap skills include stemming, long reaches, and discriminating handhold selection. Most crack climbs involve a combination of stemming, face climbing and the occasional straight-in jam. Most face climbs involve reaches and mantels between dikes. The distance between dikes and not the hold size determine route difficulty. Face climbs at Lover's Leap favor tall climbers, as a 5.10 move may be 5.9 for someone taller than 6'0" and 5.11 for someone shorter than 5'5".

You would be hard-pressed to find a granite cliff that has more large holds. This is great news if you don't want to jam your hands and feet into cracks and bad news if you take a fall, as there are many large features to break an ankle on. A Yosemite leader fall is like slipping down a granite water slide compared to The Leap, where a fall feels like traveling down a cheese grater. Or as Tad Steele says, "Lover's Leap has a strong ground up tradition—if you fall, you get ground-up."

There are few places as conducive to learning trad climbing as Lover's Leap. Most climbs are well-protected and offer rests to place gear. The downside to the huge dikes is that Lover's Leap does not teach the straight-in jamming, offwidth or thin face climbing skills needed for Yosemite or Joshua Tree. Royal Robbins makes this comparison between the Leap and Yosemite: "The opportunity to experience exposure without serious climbing difficulties means cragsmen other than experts can enjoy the thrill of steep rock and thin air. This is not so in Yosemite where there are few routes of moderate difficulty which are not low-angle, bushy, and scruffy. Steep rock in Yosemite is largely reserved for the fit warriors more interested in battle than pleasure."

Getting There

Lover's Leap rises above Highway 50 next to Strawberry, about 20 miles west of South Lake Tahoe and 30 miles east of Placerville. From Highway 50, pull into the east end of the Strawberry Lodge parking lot. The road bends left, continues another 500 feet to a bridge that crosses the American River. Immediately after the bridge, turn left and continue up a narrow road to the campground. Access most climbs from the trailhead 50 feet south of the campground bathrooms. If the campground parking is full, park west of the Strawberry Lodge in a large pullout on the south side of Highway 50. Never park on residential roads between Highway 50 or the Lover's Leap campground.

If coming from South Lake Tahoe, an alternate east parking lot offers fast access to the East Wall. Access this lot from a dirt road that is only recommended for high-clearance vehicles. (See map page 87.)

When to Climb

Lover's Leap shares Yosemite's climate, with ideal conditions in the spring and fall. The fierceness of winter decides the beginning and end of the climbing season. In lean snow years, climb from April to December. In heavy years, climb June to October.

May–June
Prime Leap season with long days and temperatures in the 60s and 70s. Depending on the snow year, the rock dries by late April. Be prepared for the occasional wet crack and storms in early May. Expect crowds.

July–August
Temperatures in the 80s and 90s make it too warm to climb in the sun, but tolerable in the shade. Bring plenty of water and wake up early (most routes get sun after noon). Seek refuge in the American River. Thunderstorms do occur (Dear John Buttress offers the only rain-protected climbing).

September–October
Fall weather is perfect with temperatures in the 60s and 70s. In early September, expect the occasional Indian summer day. Storms are rare but October nights freeze so bring warm clothes. Expect crowds.

November
Uncertain weather. The first winter storm arrives in the second or third week and may end the season. However, in a dry year the conditions are great with temperatures in the 50s and 60s and few crowds. Expect freezing nighttime temperatures.

December–March
Due to the bleak climbing conditions, nobody visits Lover's Leap in the winter. Snow covers the base and summits of most cliffs and brings freezing temperatures and wet rock. During cold snaps, the right side of the East Wall may form a rare California multi-pitch ice climb.

April
Unstable weather and snow melt usually make April too wet to climb. However, in a dry year, April has good climbing conditions and no crowds.

Twin Bridges weather—five day forecast for the closest town to The Leap: www.weather.com/weather/local/USCA1174

Chris McNamara

Bouldering

Bring the crash pad to Lover's Leap?
Yes. The 30+ campground problems
are mostly in the V1-V4 range and offer
everything from steep crimps and slopers
to long traverses and short cracks. There
are enough problems for a full day of
bouldering but most climbers just climb a
few problems after a day at the crags.

Camping

Minutes from the climbing, the
campground has all the necessities: picnic
tables, pit-toilets, privacy, drinking water,
and a bar within a 5-minute walk. The
30 campsites have 2 to 4 tents sites each
and come with one parking spot—park
additional cars on Highway 50. Each
site also has a plastic storage bin for
food storage (bring a padlock if storing
valuables). Rangers enforce the 14 total
days per year limit with fines. Carry out all
your trash and dump it at the Strawberry
Lodge for a fee or hunt in nearby city for
a dumpster. The Strawberry Lodge offers
showers for $5. Each site has a campfire
ring and you should bring your own
wood as the Forest Service discourages
collecting locally. NOTE: There have been
a few reports of climbers or campground
users forgetting the basic fire rule: Make
sure your fire is completely and totally
extinguished before you leave your site.

For free camping or if the campground is
full, you have two options:
  1) Drive to 42 Track Road, the first left
west of Strawberry Lodge. After you pass
over the bridge over Strawberry Creek you
can camp just about anywhere. Fire permits
are required for fires and are available at the
ranger station at 7887 Highway 50, Pollock
Pines; 530-644-2349.
  2) Drive 5 minutes west on Highway 50
to Wrights Lake Road. See Phantom Spires
camping section for more info (page 48).

Snakes and Critters

Rattlesnakes and squirrels are abundant at
The Leap. The East Wall squirrels wait in
the brush until you climb one pitch up—
then they strike. They chew through any
fabric, devour food, and leave your precious
pack looking like it got fed to a paper
shredder. Defend yourself against squirrel
raids: hang packs 10 feet up on the wall or
store food in Tupperware. Most active in
the spring, rattlesnakes enjoy laying out on
approach trails, descent trails, and talus.
Watch your step.

The History of Lover's Leap

Let's get the name straightened out first.
Lover's Leap is a catchy label, and it
would be a dramatic beginning to relate
a sensational story about some lovelorn
climber somersaulting down Traveler
Buttress shouting, "This will show her!" Or
was it a pair of young sweethearts, hand
in hand, failures on a 5.11, and someone
put the apostrophe in the wrong spot later?
Alas, no one seems to know the origin of
the name, so our imaginations will have to
work overtime.

  No climber set hands on this fine
cliff until the early 1950s. In those days,
Yosemite Valley was the Mecca of virtually
all Northern California cragrats and for
good reason—this is where the action was.
Not to mention, anyone who had taken
the trouble to scope out the Leap would
have noticed one arresting fact. It's hard to
believe nowadays, but once upon a time
the Leap was a filthy cliff. North facing, at
6,000 feet, and only two miles distant from
the Sierra crest, the cliff gathered nasty
winter storms. At one time, the cracks
were crammed with dirt and munge that
was wet in the spring, and dry and hard
in the summer. Bushes dotted the face. All
this would change as the pioneer climbers
arrived. The pitons and feet of the early
climbers cleansed the walls like beetles
cleansing a corpse—slow but sure. Present-
day climbers who wonder why many crack
routes were first done with aid might
wonder where they would have placed their
fingers back then.

My friend Bruce Cooke was reputed to be the first to climb at the Leap, around 1950, and he may well have done the dark slot now known as Lover's Chimney. We had other things to talk about, and I never asked him such trivial questions. The first published record of a Leap climb occurred in the 1953 annual Sierra Club Bulletin. Robin Linnett and Phil Berry (later to become a Sierra Club president) did the prominent diagonal trench on the right side of the biggest face in April 1953, and this became known as the Main Route (and, later, The Slash). They regarded their line as 1,000 feet high, proving that climbers always have (and always will) grossly exaggerate the height of new routes. In reality, the highest Leap face can't be an inch above 600 feet.

Intrigued with the Leap, Linnett and Berry established several more routes during the next few years, some of them classics, like Bear's Reach and the elegant last pitch of Bookmark. During all the days that they climbed at the cliff, they never saw another climber.

Later in 1953, Berkeley climber Frank DeSaussure and a friend struggled up the sinister gash just left of the tallest Leap wall, naming it Eeyore's Ecstasy (as older folk know, Eeyore was the crabby donkey in the classic kid's book Winnie the Pooh). This dank, claustrophobic route was not fated to become popular, but around the same time Sacramento climber Ken Edsburg put up a route destined to become one of the truly sublime moderate routes in the United States: Corrugation Corner. The name is perfect, for the rock, as elsewhere on much of the Leap, is, well, corrugated. And the corner itself is gigantic and right-angled—you will not mistake it for a face or an arête. It's amazing to me that the route didn't gain instant popularity, but I would guess that few people, besides Edsburg and his cronies, did the route for the next decade. No write-up in a magazine. No guidebook available. These facts, of course, helped keep the route unknown.

Not much route activity took place for the remainder of the 1950s. I well remember that on one of my first visits, in May 1960, I had a choice of only eight or ten established routes, most known solely by word of mouth. I did most of these over the Memorial Day Weekend, but instantly returned to Yosemite Valley, not giving the Leap another thought for six years. Why I didn't stick around and put up some new routes is incomprehensible now, but I suppose the dirt and short routes didn't call out to me.

The 1960s were uneventful as well. In June 1963, Edsburg and Jack Davidson attacked the biggest face of the Leap, just to the right of Corrugation Corner. This two-day climb, soon simply named the North Face Route, became, in a Summit Magazine article, the second journalistic account of the Leap. In those days, Summit was the only mag in the U.S. to deal with rock climbing and was widely read by cragrats. The words of the author, Davidson, may have been the signal that began the Leap's popularity. He wrote: "We hoped in the future more climbers would discover the many climbing possibilities of this great place." Not the most eloquent words, perhaps, but surely a clarion call to California climbers.

And they came. The late 1960s saw a huge surge of activity. The Line was nailed in 1965 by TM Herbert and Doug Tompkins—the rating was given as 5.5, A3. The perfect cracks so familiar to us nowadays were clogged with dirt, and, obviously, even the aid climbing was difficult. Traveler Buttress was done free in 1966 from talus to summit, perhaps the first 5.9 at the Leap. The name, for which I admit responsibility, demands that I tell an obscure tale. Pink rock near the crux jamcrack reminded me of the word "pinko," once a pejorative for a communist. Pinko didn't seem like a suitable name, so my then-fertile brain conjured up "fellow traveler," another name for a commie rat. This seemed too cumbersome, so minutes later I had it: Traveler Buttress. Now it's often called Traveler, which changes the original meaning entirely. So it goes. A grand climb, in any case.

Edsburg and Herbert were the main honchos of the mid and late 1960s, but

Gordie Webster, Steve Thompson, Dick Long, and Warren Harding all played important roles in establishing new routes. From about 1967 to 1971, Royal Robbins took time off from Yosemite and ran a climbing school at the Leap. He put up many new routes, and introduced countless clients to the joys of climbing vertical rock. The first guide to the Leap, done by me, appeared in the 1967 Ascent and undoubtedly attracted hordes of climbers during the following years. No longer would you be alone on the cliffs on a weekend, and soon even the weekdays would ring with the sound of "Off belay!"

Before I leave the 1960s, I should mention two watershed climbs. Tom Higgins, best known for his balls-out routes in Tuolumne, climbed The Line free with Frank Sarnquist in 1968. True, much of the crud had been gouged out of the cracks by repeated piton placements and removal, but these two climbers, among the best of their time, established a free route that is to this day my favorite short route in California. And, obviously, not a trace of dirt remains after many thousands of ascents. This ascent proved that steep free climbing was possible anywhere on the formation and from this moment on extremely little aid climbing was done. Today there are only a few aid routes.

The second event concerns Jeff Lowe, the finest ice climber of his generation—and not a bad rock climber either! In 1969 he soloed, on a frigid April day, in winter conditions, the Hourglass Wall, a 5.9, A2 effort unimaginable to most.

Robbins was responsible for several bold routes in the early 1970s. I once had to follow him up a loose and desperate line we named Incubus. Even he struggled. (He later wrote: "nightmarish Incubus, a savage route.") As follower, I often fell and grabbed the rope and cursed Royal's forebears. Now the route is rated 10b with a death-fall X added for good measure. That fellow was a genius, for sure. His other route, done in 1973 with the acclaimed Brit, Ken Wilson, is a far better one. With bold and complex climbing, Fantasia is not done by the meek,

even today. Robbins wrote an avant-garde account of this climb in his book *Advanced Rockcraft*. Of the region immediately above the initial arch, where the difficulties begin instantly, Robbins had this to say: "It is an area where technical competence combined with 'attack,' if freed from the chain of prudence, can easily lead to becoming airborne."

Virtually all of the classic routes described below were first done in the fifteen-year period from 1963 to 1978, the Golden Age of climbing at the Leap. TM Herbert was one of the most active first-ascentionists, putting up five of these classics. Oddly enough, all these lay on the far eastern wall. (Scared of steep rock, TM?) Ken Edsburg and Jerry Sublette often climbed at the Leap during this period, and established such routes as Surrealistic Pillar, East Wall, and Haystack. Jay Smith and his buddies came along in the mid 1970s and free-climbed the fabulous Hospital Corner, among other accomplishments.

– Steve Roper

Daily Climbing Itineraries

The following are some possible itineraries for your Lover's Leap trip. Each itinerary focuses on a certain difficulty range so that you can best plan your trip around your climbing ability.

5.5 and 5.6 Day

Head to the Hogsback and start on **Knapsack Crack (5.5, 3 pitches)**. Move over to **Manic Depressive (5.5, 2 pitches)** and consider belaying at the bolts on the right and toproping **Wave Rider (5.6, 2 pitches)**. Next, climb **Harvey's Wallbangers, Center (5.6, 2 pitches)** followed by **Deception (5.6, 3 pitches)**. If you still have time, consider moving over to the Lower Buttress and climbing **The Farce (5.5, 2 pitches)**.

5.7 Day

Start on the Lower Buttress and acquaint yourself with The Leap's unique dikes and cracks on **The Farce (5.5, 2 pitches)**. Next, climb **Pop Bottle (5.7, 3 pitches)**, a great introduction to the East Wall. Then, move right to the route **East Wall (5.7, 3 pitches)**,

The Leap's best introductory three-pitch climb. Finish off the day with **Bear's Reach** (5.7, 3 pitches), the East Wall's most sustained and quality 5.7.

Or

Climb the best 5.7 link-up at Lover's Leap: start with **Surrealistic Pillar** (5.7, 3 pitches) and from the top, walk up to the Main Wall and climb **Corrugation Corner** (5.7, 3 pitches). This is many people's favorite Lover's Leap outing. For this link-up, climb with just your approach shoes and a small day pack with food and water. Start at dawn, and if you really want to avoid crowds, climb Corrugation Corner first and return to Surrealistic Pillar in the late afternoon.

5.8 Day
The Groove (5.8, 2 pitches) is the best introduction to 5.8 at The Leap and a great warm up for the longer 5.8 routes on the East Wall such as **Haystack** (5.8, 3 pitches). This is Lover's Leap's most striking 5.8 and takes one of the most most obvious lines on the face. Move next to the more sustained and exposed **East Crack** (5.8, 3 pitches) which will leave you well prepared to break into the 5.9 realm. When Haystack is crowded, usually East Crack is not until the last pitch where other routes converge.

5.9 Day
For a more challenging Lower Buttress/ Main Wall link-up, climb **The Groove** (5.8, 2 pitches) and, from the top, hike up to The Leap's longest and wildest 5.9, **Traveler Buttress** (5.9, 4 pitches). For the most challenging link-up that puts you in "easy" 5.10 terrain, start with **Surrealistic Pillar Direct** (5.10a, 3 pitches) followed by Traveler Buttress. After the descent, if you reach the East Wall at the right time in the afternoon, **The Line** (5.9, 3 pitches) may be free of crowds. This route must be climbed by every 5.9 climber.

Or

For a burly and frightening 5.9 day, start on **Psychedelic Tree** (5.9, 4 pitches). The loose blocks and sustained moves will get your head ready for **Scimitar** (5.9 R, 3 pitches). In turn, the mild runout and challenging moves on this climb will prepare you for **Fantasia** (5.9 R, 3 pitches), one of the best (and more runout) climbs at The Leap.

5.10 Day
Begin on **Surrealistic Pillar Direct** (5.10a, 3 pitches) and either climb all three pitches or set up a toprope at the anchors for **Surrealistic Pillar Direct Variation** (5.10d, 1 pitch). Climb to the top of Lower Buttress and walk up to the Main Ledge and climb **Hospital Corner** (5.10a, 2 pitches). With a 70m rope, you can toprope laps on the incredible second pitch stemming corner. Next, descend to Tombstone Ledge and climb **Tombstone Terror** (5.10c, 1 pitch), possibly The Leap's best short 5.10 route.

Dream Lover's Leap Climbing Day
The ultimate Lover's Leap day would link together the three significant walls: Lower Buttress, Main Wall and East Wall. It might look like this: Start on **Surrealistic Pillar** (5.7, 3 pitches) and continue up to **Corrugation Corner** (5.7, 3 pitches). Descend to the East Wall, and move left to right climbing **Haystack** (5.8, 3 pitches), **Bear's Reach** (5.7, 3 pitches), and **The Line** (5.9, 3 pitches). Because all of these routes are extremely popular, the link-up is probably only practical on a deserted late fall or early spring day.

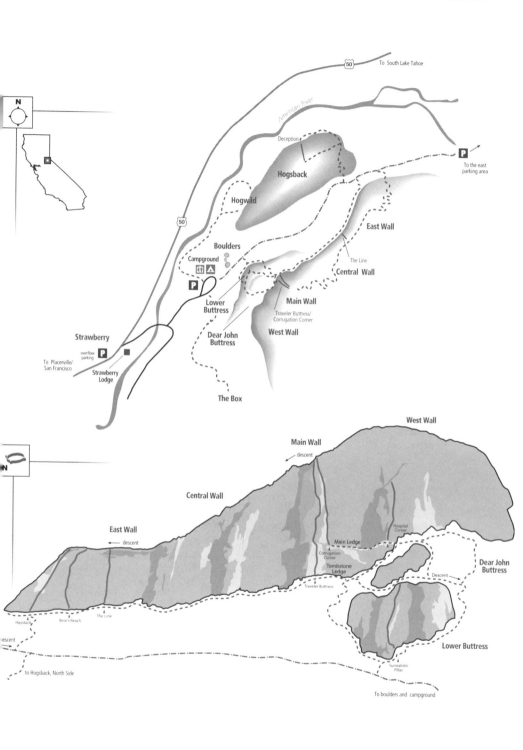

East Wall

Approach time: **10-15 minutes**

Sun exposure: **noon to afternoon**

Height of routes: **350–430'**

The East Wall is a moderate trad climber's dream. Irresistible four and five-star 5.7-5.9 routes cover the wall at 50-foot intervals and offer a mixture of striking cracks and featured face climbs. If the East Wall had only two routes it would be worthwhile. The fact that it has more than 20 classic climbs makes it one of the best moderate granite crags in the United States. To top it off, the East Wall has one of the easiest descents you will find off of any 400-foot face. A good thing, too, because once you top out on one climb, you will want to run back to the base and climb another.

Approach

The approach is mostly flat and takes 10-15 minutes from the campground or 5 minutes from the east parking lot. From 50 feet east of the campground bathrooms, take the Old Pony Express Trail (the main trail) east. After 5-10 minutes and once even with Haystack at the left side of the East Wall, turn right onto a climbers' trail. Another few hundred feet of trail and talus puts you at the base.

Descent

The descent takes 10-15 minutes. From the top of any route, walk away from the edge for 10-50 feet and pick up a climbers' trail that switchbacks down to the northeast. Reach the Old Pony Express Trail and turn left. A hike of 100 yards puts you back in front of the East Wall.

A. Pop Bottle   5.7★★

FA: Gene Drake, Mark Haymond, Larry Morris, 9/69.

With just a few moves of 5.7, Pop Bottle is a great introduction to the East Wall. While the route ascends lower-angle rock, a few steep bulges add some spice. Originally rated 5.6, the route became harder after rock fall.

The crux comes 50 feet off the ground and requires an awkward reach over a roof to a hidden hold. Belay at the golden rock scar if you want to see and hear your partner. After the gold scar comes the second crux. Climb on face holds (5.6) to the right of the difficulties, head straight up on steep 5.7 jams, or reach left in the corner to keep it 5.6. The big ledge lacks solid cracks and only a few decent belay options exist (save some medium cams). Another option is to belay 20 feet before the ledge on small gear. You can escape left on 3rd class and a few 5.1 moves.

The second pitch starts with a boulder problem followed by a few slightly runout face moves. The climbing then eases to 4th class at which point either walk off left or continue up and right on low-angle terrain to the two-bolt second pitch anchor. Climb the third pitch if you must stand on the top of the wall. This pitch does not challenge or inspire.

Micro Brew (not shown)   5.8★★

FA: Steve Stroscheim, 1996.

A 50-foot thin diagonal crack that comes into East Corner from the left.

B. East Corner   5.11b★★★

FA: TM Herber, Bob Kamps, 1969.

Sustained 5.7 first pitch—a good escape from crowds. Second pitch climbs the big corner to a devious 5.11b roof boulder problem. The crux requires more finesse than brute strength and can be well-protected from a marginal stance. With the exception of the crux, the second pitch is 5.10a and it's common for 5.10 climbers to pull through that single 5.11 move on gear.

C. Haystack   5.8★★★★★

FA: Ken Edsburg, TM Herbert, Jerry Sublette, 1965.

Second to The Line, Haystack takes one of the most striking crack systems on the East Wall and ascends a diversity of terrain from straight-in jamming to face moves and roofs, Haystack is defined by a wild 4-foot roof move on the second pitch. With only two short crux sections, this is a great intro to the 5.8 realm.

The first pitch warms you up with easy 5th class moves that lead to a few 5.6 jams to the belay. The second pitch starts with a 5.8 stem and finger jam crux that leads to the wild 5.8 roof. When climbed perfectly, the roof feel like 5.7, but done wrong the roof feels like 5.10. The roof eats ropes so place a cam at the lip so the rope runs cleanly. An optional belay 20 feet above the roof allows the leader to keep watch of the follower through the crux. Save a 3-inch cam for the standard belay.

The third pitch follows a big corner through a series of small, fun bulges. A 50m rope barely makes it to the top. This pitch easily breaks into two pitches with two options to bail out left if storms threaten.

D. Preparation H   5.8★★★★

FA: M. Haymond, Jim Hicks, 1969.

Sustained fingers, face, and bulges with a cool hand crack finish. A more challenging and better quality start to Haystack.

E. Fantasia   5.9 R★★★★★

FA: Royal Robbins, Ken Wilson, 5/73.

Described by first ascensionist Ken Wilson as "more bold than hard," Fantasia is the Leap's best runout climb. Unlike Tuolumne or Yosemite runouts on low-angle desperate smears, Fantasia climbs a steep wall studded with large holds. With few large features, routefinding is difficult and gets harder the higher you climb. Gear comes at 20 to 40-foot intervals.

Originally, the route had no bolts. Royal Robbins led the first pitch and belayed off two Lost Arrow pitons hand-placed behind a fragile flake (below the current bolted anchor). Why? Said Royal, "I thought that, coming from the British school of clean-climbing, Ken would approve of the novel piton placements. But when he arrived at the belay, he made it clear he didn't approve at all."

Chris McNamara

On the first pitch, sling every piece and watch rope drag. An unprotected 5.6 move 40 feet off the deck leads to the first gear placement. The 5.9 reachy crux comes 15 feet below the anchors and 15 feet above your last gear.

Ten feet up the second pitch, tie off a mediocre knob and continue up and left on steep dikes. Eventually move back right to a 5.8 bulge and leaning corner. Don't go too far left and join Fear No Evil (5.9 R) or Haystack.

The devious last pitch has many options. The easiest way steps left and to a fixed pin. Continue up and right underclinging a leaning corner to the routefinding crux. Decently protected 5.10b goes straight over the roof. For more moderate 5.9 moves, pull the roof further right. From here, generally go straight up and pull roofs left of the big green lichen-covered roof. Break the last pitch into two if you have bad rope drag or poor communication with your belayer.

F. Scimitar   5.9★★★★

FA: Mike Covington, Dick Erb, 6/69.
FFA: Jim Orey, F. Van Overbeck, 1972.

Scimitar is almost as good as Fantasia but without the consistent runouts. This climb has it all: lieback cracks, runout face, and steep bulges. While the general route line is obvious, finding the easiest crux sequences is tricky.

On the first pitch 5.9 crux, lieback and stem the left corner or work more awkward stemming in the right corner. You have a few options on how to negotiate the 40-foot 5.6 runout at the start of the second pitch. In general, diagonal up and right. The wild last pitch climbs a steep maze of overlaps. Be creative; circuitous face climbing is sometimes easier than using the crack. Near the finish there is an easy escape route out right.

G. East Crack   5.8★★★

FA: TM Herbert, Gordon Webster, 1966.

East Crack provides a variety of sustained 5.7 and 5.8 terrain. Because the route doesn't have a memorable crux, it sees little traffic relative to Bear's Reach or East Wall. With only a few 5.8 moves, this is a good

entry to 5.8 and is only moderately more difficult (and better protected) than Bear's Reach.

The first pitch is straightforward with one 5.7 move around the roof. The second pitch is the business: face and crack moves lead to two steep, awkward, and well protected 5.8 bulges. When crowded, belay on the far left side and high on Bushy Ledge.

The final pitch features a distinct 5.7 crux that requires stemming on poor footholds while reaching high into a 3-inch crack for a hidden incut jug. Just before the top, either set gear for a directional and escape right or continue straight up the wild 5.9 mantel variation. Belay before reaching the rim for best communication with your follower.

H. Bear's Reach   5.7★★★★★

FA: Phil Berry, Robin Linnett, 1956.

This must-do climb offers more than a few memorable face and crack moves. The name comes from the second pitch crux where, depending on your height, you must make a huge "Bear's Reach" between two large holds. The first half of the climb links together a variety of short cracks with face moves while the second half follows a series of corners. Just shy of runout, this climb is recommended for confident 5.7 leaders.

The first pitch is the most serious on the climb. After getting gear 10 feet up, you must go 15 feet to the next gear. Save the bigger cams for the large steep flake at the end of the pitch. The comfy belay ledge is surrounded by dangerously hollow rock and a climber died when his anchor pulled. Back up the belay with gear up high and left, then wedge your rump firmly in the ledge.

Exhilarating face and flake moves on Pitch 2. Place pro at every opportunity, especially in the first 30 feet before the namesake Bear's Reach. Here, with pro at your feet, either deadpoint to a jug or face climb up small holds. When setting the belay at "(Once a) Bushy Ledge," keep in mind that other climbers may join you from converging routes. For the third pitch beta, see East Crack.

A. Pop Bottle 5.7★★ nuts: 1-2 sets; cams: 1-2 ea .6-3.5"
B. East Corner 5.11b★★★ nuts: 1-2 sets; cams: 1-2 ea .5-2"
C. Haystack 5.8★★★★★ nuts: 1-2 sets; cams: 1-2 ea .6-3.5"
D. Preparation H 5.8★★★★ nuts: 1-2 sets; cams: 2 ea .5-2.5"
E. Fantasia 5.9 R★★★★★ nuts: 1 set; cams: 1 ea .5-2.5"
F. Scimitar 5.9★★★ nuts: 1-2 sets; cams: 1-2 ea .5-3.5"

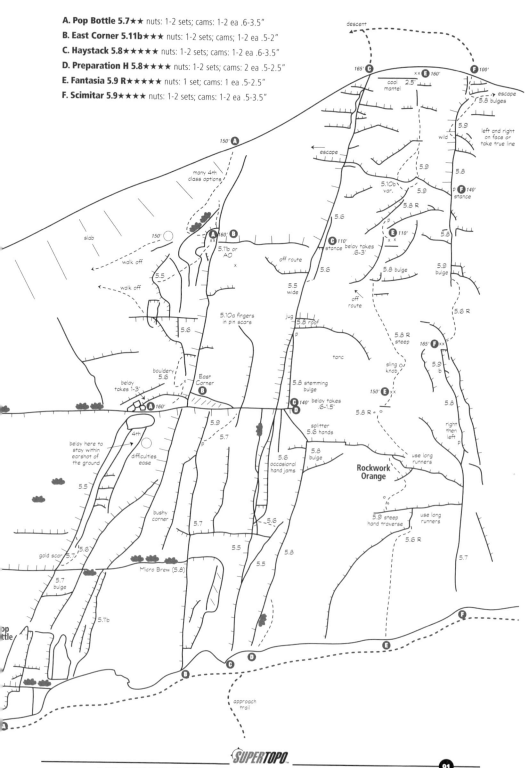

I. East Wall   5.7★★★

FA: Ken and Mike Edsburg, Jerry Sublette, 1964.

This adventurous climb ascends an enormous featured corner before meandering left on wild dikes. Because of the difficult routefinding and exposed moves, this is recommended for experienced 5.7 leaders.

On the first pitch, stem a big corner with many parallel cracks and great gear.

The second pitch is the psychological and routefinding crux. Traverse left around the corner, climb up and then left into a large left-leaning flake system. Here, there is a highly recommended, but terrifyingly exposed 5.7 or 5.6 traverse left (use slings on all gear). The standard route continues up the large flake system then moves left to a belay just before Bushy Ledge (belay on Bushy Ledge when not crowded).

J. End of the Line   5.10c★★

FA: Jay Smith, Karl McConachie, Paul Crawford, 1984.

This one-pitch route passes the time when stuck at the end of The Line. With at least five 5.10 face and crack cruxes, the climb feels much longer than its 70 feet. With few large dikes, End of The Line requires good finger jamming technique. There is barely enough gear in the first 30 feet to prevent you from decking, so make sure you are a confident 5.10 leader.

Start directly or traverse in from the left (both variations are 5.10). After 30 feet of attention-grabbing 5.10 crack and face moves, the terrain eases before the grand finale: three well-protected 5.10 face moves between big rests. The 5.10c crux features an improbable high-step with a bolt at your waist.

K. The Line   5.9★★★★★

FA: TM Herbert, Doug Tompkins, 1966.
FFA: Tom Higgins, Frank Sarnquist, 1968.

The Line is the most popular and striking route at Lover's Leap. The name says it all: the climb follows an obvious plumb line up the center of the East Wall. The name also speaks to the three or more climbers you usually wait behind. The Line offers a delicious mixture of lieback, stem, and face moves with the occasional straight-in jam. After thousands of ascents, the rock has been buffed to perfection—no dirt or grit here. Paul Piana summed up the climb nicely: "Best 5.9 I've ever done. Great protection after the first 20 feet. Hold up a rack and it sucks in a nut."

Royal Robbins describes the first pitch as "the best pitch at The Leap, and one of the ten best pitches I have done anywhere." The powerful 5.9 crux of The Line comes mercifully just 20 feet off the ground. From there, the first pitch remains sustained for another 130 feet to the belay. Luckily, several stances give ample opportunity to place pro and shake out. There are a few belay options but, if there are people behind you, belay high.

The second pitch is long and sustained with the occasional awkward crux and short runout. Stem as much as possible and be patient at the crux 5.9 bulge.

The third pitch turns a wild 5.8 roof on big holds to unrelenting exposure to the rim.

L. Labor of Love   5.10a★★

FA: Kadas, et al.

A splendid dike climbing odyssey… if you are tall. The crux is height dependent: 5.9 if taller than 6'0", 5.10c if 5'9" to 5'11", and 5.11 if 5'8" or shorter. There is a bolt at the crux. However, the other bolts, especially the last, are usually 5-10 feet below a hard move. The holds are big and secure on the few 15-foot runouts. A good consolation when the The Line is too crowded. Bring a second rope to rappel.

Deviate (not shown)   5.8 R★★★★

FA: Ben Borson, Tom Higgins, 1968.

Maybe the best 5.8 R at The Leap. Start 30 feet left of Psychedelic Tree below a small roof located 25 feet off the ground. Pull the roof into a discontinuous crack. Best to climb one 200-foot pitch to the ledge.

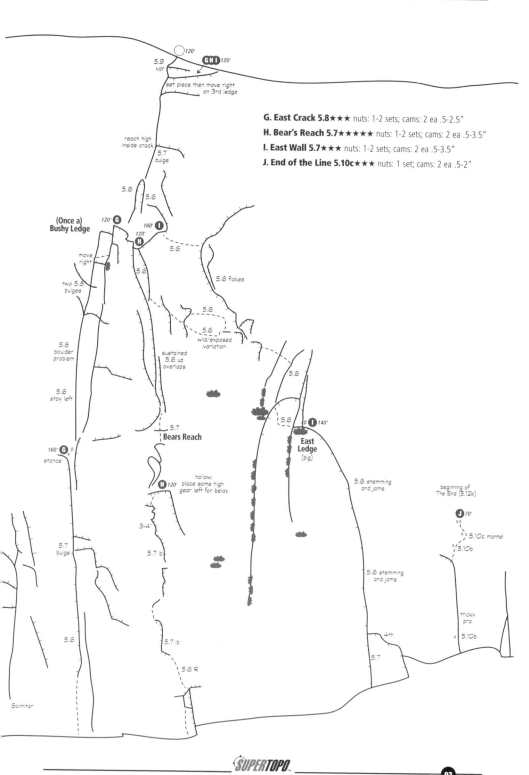

○ 120'

5.9 var

G H I 120'

set piece then move right on 3rd ledge

G. **East Crack 5.8★★★** nuts: 1-2 sets; cams: 2 ea .5-2.5"

H. **Bear's Reach 5.7★★★★★** nuts: 1-2 sets; cams: 2 ea .5-3.5"

I. **East Wall 5.7★★★** nuts: 1-2 sets; cams: 2 ea .5-3.5"

J. **End of the Line 5.10c★★★** nuts: 1 set; cams: 2 ea .5-2"

reach high inside crack

5.7 bulge

5.6

5.6

(Once a) Bushy Ledge

120' **G**

160' **I**

120' **H**

5.6

move right

5.6

two 5.8 bulges

5.6 flakes

5.8 boulder problem

5.6

5.6 wild/exposed variation

sustained 5.6 up overlaps

5.6 stay left

5.6

5.6

5.6

p **I** 140'

5.7

Bears Reach

160' **G** p

stance

East Ledge (big)

hollow: place some high gear left for belay

H 120'

5.6 stemming and jams

beginning of The End (5.12b)

J 70'

xx

x 5.10c mantel

x 5.10b

3-4"

5.7 bulge

5.7 lb

5.6 stemming and jams

tricky pro

x 5.10b

5.6

5.7 lb

4th

5.7

5.6 R

Scimitar

M. Psychedelic Tree   5.9★★

FA: Bruce Cooke and TM Herbert, 1968.
FFA: Rick Sumner, 6/75.

When most East Wall routes have four or more climbers apiece, there is often no line on Psychedelic Tree. Here's why: 1) The route is sustained at 5.8 and 5.9 and 2) fewer ascents mean more dirt and loose blocks. Psychedelic Tree is the The Line's uglier sibling: it's as direct but has more munge and loose blocks. To its credit, it has a more dramatic finish than The Line.

Climb this route in two long pitches, three medium pitches, or four short ones. The four-pitch way is described below.

The first pitch features enormous blocks that are apparently held in by few grains of dirt. Pull on the blocks to make the climbing easy but terrifying, or stem for harder moves and piece of mind. Belay at a small ledge after 130 feet or earlier.

The second pitch starts with a tricky wide crack move which, lacking dikes, requires crack jamming technique. Belay on the huge ledge.

The third pitch includes an awkward 5.9 high step followed by more 5.8 to the Psychedelic Tree.

For the fourth pitch, early climbers shimmied up the tree, then stepped across to the summit. However, the tree is losing branches and is unprotected. Better to climb the 5.9 mantel finish, the most spectacular top-out at Lover's Leap.

N. Unnamed   5.10a★★★

FA: unknown

Twenty feet of 5.6 to first bolt. Well-protected face leads past another three bolts to crack finish. Can toprope this and a left variation with a 60m rope.

Chris McNamara

Todd Offenbacher stretches through the crux on Pitch 1 of Fantasia.

K. The Line 5.9★★★★★ nuts: 1-2 sets; cams: 2 ea .6-3"

L. Labor of Love 5.10a★★★ nuts: 1 set; cams: 2 ea .6-2"

M. Psychadelic Tree 5.9★★ nuts: 1-2 sets; cams: 2 ea .6-3.5", 1 ea 4.5" (optional)

N. Unnamed 5.10a★★★ cams: 2 ea .6-2.5"

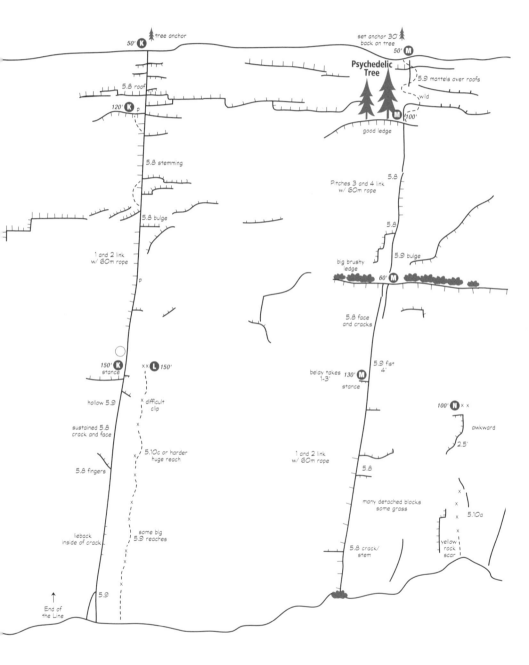

Central Wall

Approach time: **20 minutes**

Sun exposure: **afternoon to sunset**

Height of routes: **500'**

The Central Wall is as steep and dramatic as the East Wall or Main Wall, but has few crowds. When there are 40 people on the East Wall, the more adventurous and intimidating Central Wall is often empty.

Chris McNamara

Approach

Pick up the Old Pony Express Trail 50 feet east of the campground bathrooms. After 5-10 minutes, and once even with Haystack at the left side of the East Wall, turn right onto a climbers' trail. Another few hundred feet on trail and talus puts you at the base of the East Wall. Follow the base trail for a few hundred yards to the base of the Central Wall.

Descent

Allow 20 minutes to walk from the finish of Eagle Buttress to the Old Pony Express Trail. From the finish, walk 50 feet away from the edge and find a climbers' trail that switchbacks down to the northeast. The obvious trail meanders 50-200 feet away and parallel to the edge. Reach the Old Pony Express Trail and turn left.

A. Lover's Chimney   5.7★★

FA: Bruce Cooke, 1949.

The first Lover's Leap climb. It's a sometimes dirty and brushy event for those who seek adventure, not clean cracks. The first pitch has an awkward 5.6 chimney crux. The wild second pitch enters a cave and ascends a chimney and chockstones to a bushy ledge. Continue over bushes and 3rd class, then escape left via a wild stemming move to a bushy ledge. The final pitch moves out left onto a cool 5.5

arête before going back up and right on a somewhat dirty gully. The last part of the pitch involves a wild 5.6 stem to escape the gully.

B. Bookmark   5.8★★★

FA: Steve Thompson, Gordon Webster, 1966.
Above Main Ledge: P. Berry, R Linnet, 1954.

This semi-obscure local favorite features a 5.8 offwidth crux. On the first pitch climb left of the main crack, then move right into the crack to some cool handjams. Climb a full 200 feet to a ledge or belay at 150 feet on a stance. The second pitch climbs a cool orange-ish corner with a polished wide crack at midway. Protect the crux offwidth/chimney moves with thin nuts on the left wall.

C. Roofer Madness   5.10d★★★★

FA: Jay Smith, Rick Sumner, 1977.

The crux comes 10 feet off the ground pulling a short, bouldery roof. Sustained climbing to the anchors. The second pitch has two starts: a direct 5.10c roof, or 5.8 face moves around the bulge to the right and then back left into the main crack. The crack widens and remains sustained to the

Main Ledge. Combine the first and second pitches for an awesome 5.11a link-up. Either rappel to the ground or continue up Eagle Buttress, Right.

Chopper Madness (not shown) 5.11a★★★

FA: Petch Pietrolungo, 2002.

Sustained thin crack to the right of Roofer Madness.

D. Eagle Buttress, Right 5.10a★★★★

FA: TM Herbert, Gordon Webster, 1966.

This unsung classic escaped notice for many years. The climbing is sustained, juggy, and sometimes spectacularly exposed. Stem on large dikes with great protection in nearby cracks. Bring 10-15 slings and plan to use one on almost every piece to reduce rope drag.

The first 20 feet of the first pitch involve sparsely protected dike moves (search hard for gear). If rope drag gets you, belay mid-pitch on the detached block.

On the second pitch, climb up and right toward a knob (lasso this from the ledge for protection). Make a 5.9 hand traverse right under a small roof, then climb sloping 5.9 dikes. Belay at an incredibly exposed stance with two bolts.

On Pitch 3, stem (don't jam) the many cruxes. 3.5-4.5" cams protect the middle of the pitch. Use many slings or rope drag will strain you at the 5.10a high crux. When in doubt, reach high for a dike and stem.

Pitches 4 and 5 are mostly 4th class with an occasional harder move. Both pitches link only by running out most of Pitch 4.

Chris McNamara

Sarah Felchlin stoked on the large dikes of Surrealistic Pillar.

A. Lover's Chimney 5.7★★ cams: 1-2 ea .5-3"
B. Bookmark 5.8★★★ cams: 1-2 ea .6-4.5"

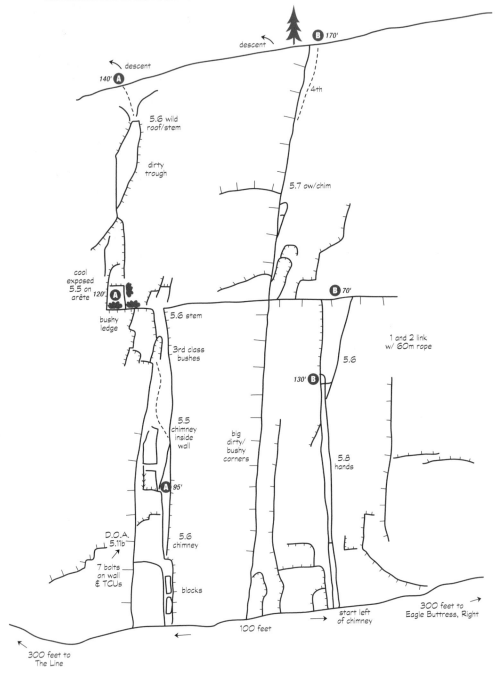

descent

🅑 170'

descent

🅐 140'

5.6 wild
roof/stem

4th

dirty
trough

5.7 ow/chim

cool
exposed
5.5 on
arête 120' 🅐

🅑 70'

bushy
ledge

5.6 stem

1 and 2 link
w/ 60m rope

3rd class
bushes

5.6

130' 🅑

5.5
chimney
inside
wall

big
dirty/
bushy
corners

5.8
hands

🅐 95'

D.O.A.
5.11b

5.6
chimney

7 bolts
on wall
& TCUs

blocks

start left
of chimney

300 feet to
Eagle Buttress, Right

100 feet

300 feet to
The Line

C. Roofer Madness 5.10d ★★★★
nuts: 1-2 sets; cams: 2 ea .6-3.5"

D. Eagle Buttress, Right 5.10a ★★★★
nuts: 1-2 sets; cams: 2 ea .6-3.5", 1 ea 4.5" (optional)

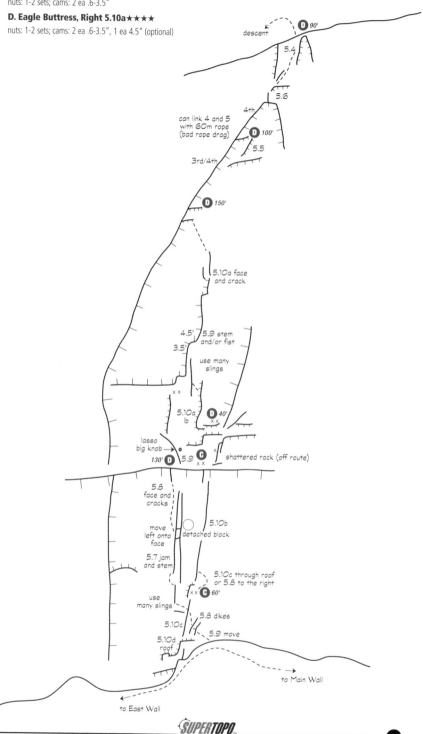

Main Wall and West Wall

Approach time: **15-25 minutes**

Sun exposure: **noon to afternoon**

Height of routes: **500'**

The Main Wall appears taller than its 500 feet and all the climbs look 5.12. Fortunately, looks are deceiving and like all Leap climbs, huge dikes and good handholds allow a handful of well-protected and relatively moderate climbs to sneak up the imposing face. Once on the rock, you notice a cruel little trick: the steep slope below makes the climbing feel more exposed than it is. All this means one thing: The Main Wall is irresistible.

Approach

Pick up the Old Pony Express Trail 50 feet east of the campground bathrooms. After a few hundred yards, when perpendicular to the Lower Buttress, turn right onto a climbers' trail. After 100 yards you reach the base of the Lower Buttress. Turn left on a faint climbers' trail that skirts the base. After a steep 100 yards the trail angles left and moves into some small talus in a drainage. A faint trail winds its way toward the Main Wall and joins a more defined climbers' trail before the Lower Main Wall. For Tombstone Terror and the first pitch of Traveler Buttress, move up and left onto Tombstone Ledge. For all other Main Wall routes, follow the trail up and right for 100 yards until you gain the Main Ledge and can move back left.

As an alternate approach that causes less erosion, walk the Old Pony Express Trail until you pass a large tree that fell across the trail and was cut

out. Thirty feet farther is a trail that leads up the talus directly to Main Wall.

If climbing Traveler Buttress or Corrugation Corner, approach with only the gear, food, and water you need on the climb. If you pack heavy and leave extra stuff at the base, plan on spending an extra 45 minutes after the climb to recover it.

Descent

Allow 20 minutes from the summit to the Old Pony Express Trail then another 10 minutes back to the campground. From the finish, find the climbers' trail that heads east and parallel with the edge of the cliff. Hike for 10-15 minutes, eventually joining the East Wall descent to the Old Pony Express Trail. NOTE: Descending west from the summit seems faster but this way is tricky and not recommended.

Chris McNamara staying above ground on R.I.P. (Casey McTaggart)

Chris McNamara

TOMBSTONE LEDGE

A. R.I.P   5.11d★★★★★

FA: unknown

Great quality thin moves get continuously steeper and harder. Can toprope after climbing Tombstone Terror and lowering down to the anchors.

B. Tombstone Terror   5.10c★★★★★

FA: Gary Anderson, Steve Miller, Jay Smith, Rick Sumner, 1976.

This may be the best 5.10c pitch at Lover's Leap. Strenuous lieback and stem moves on perfect rock. Move fast and don't stall. The route's name comes from the unprotected first 15 feet where a fall would result in an unpleasant landing on the tombstones. Most climbers stop at the first anchor and rappel back to the ground (a great toprope with a 60m rope). The second pitch is 5.7.

C. Boothill   5.11a★★★★★

FA: Paul Crawford, Paul Obanheim, and Jay Smith, 1984.

The best 5.11a face at The Leap. Steep and immaculate white rock. Can easily toprope after climbing Tombstone Terror or the first part of Traveler Buttress and traversing left. Originally a scary lead on fixed pitons and one bolt.

D. Traveler Buttress   5.9★★★★★

FA: (below Main Ledge) Steve Roper, Steve Thompson, and Gordon Webster, 1966. (above Main Ledge) unknown.
FFA: (above Main Ledge) Dick Long and Allen Steck, 1965.

Traveler Buttress is one of the most varied Leap routes. It delivers steep face, straight-in cracks, a burly offwidth, and runout dike-hiking. It's included in Roper and Steck's *50 Classic Climbs of North America* and according to Royal Robbins, "Personally, I think it's the best route at Lover's Leap. It takes first place for quality of climbing, variety, situation, and length."

Don't bypass the first pitch by traversing in high on the Main Ledge. You will miss a steep 5.8 dike journey and a thought provoking flared jamming 5.8 crux. Falls from here have resulted in injury.

On the notorious second pitch, the dikes vanish to leave a smooth and holdless 20-foot 5.9 offwidth. The 5.10b R variation on the left is heads-up. Bring a 4.5" cam, search for hand jams, and grovel. Higher, the crack narrows to a fantastic hand crack.

The third pitch climbs one of the most exposed arête's at Lover's Leap before turning to lower-angle but runout dike hiking. Finding a spot to belay can be tricky. The last pitch continues up mostly moderate dikes to the rim.

E. Silly Willy Crack   5.12c★★★★

FA: Bill Price, 1982.

A pumpy 5.11 finger crack leads to a rest and then a steeper and more pumpy 5.12c finger/lieback crack. Usually toproped with a 60m rope after leading half of the first pitch of Traveler Buttress. Gets great evening light.

A. R.I.P 5.11d ★★★★★ 7 draws
B. Tombstone Terror 5.10c ★★★★★ cams: 2 ea .4-2"
C. Boothill 5.11a ★★★★★ 7 draws
D. Traveler Buttress 5.9 ★★★★★ nuts: 1 set; cams: 2 ea .5-3.5", 1 ea 4.5", 1 ea 7" (optional)
E. Silly Willy Crack 5.12c ★★★★ nuts: 1 set; cams: 3 ea .4-1"

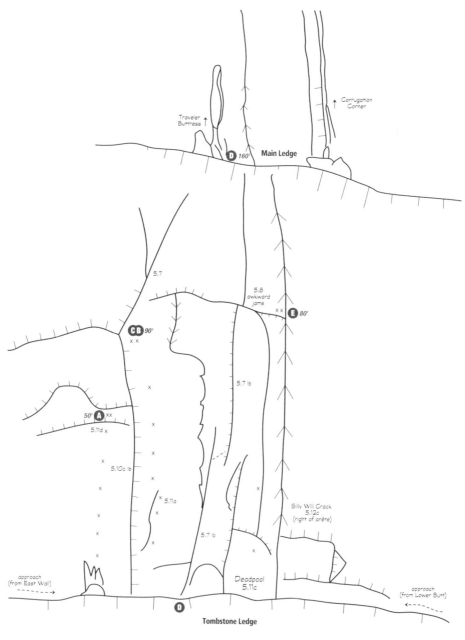

MAIN LEDGE

F. Corrugation Corner   5.7★★★★★

FA: Kurt Edsburg, et al, early 1960s.

From a distance Corrugation Corner
looks like a low-angle weakness in the
otherwise steep Main Wall. In reality it's
one of the steepest granite 5.7s anywhere.
Instead of following the main corner,
the route often climbs a horrendously
exposed arête. The cruxes are technically
5.7, but psychologically they often feel
much harder. Royal Robbins said this, "…
the Corner still rates first place because of
its magnificence as a corner; both from a
distance and close up it is an elegant piece
of rock architecture." This may be the best
climb at Lover's Leap and it has the crowds
to prove it. Approach the climb early and
prepare yourself to wait behind slower
climbers. The variations throughout the
climb unfortunately do not help you to pass
slower climbers.

The pitch warms you up with sustained
5.6 stemming, a bulge, and then a fun hand
traverse right. Miss the hand traverse and
you're in 5.9 offwidth terrain.

The second pitch is one of the steepest
and most intimidating 5.7 pitches
anywhere. A stemming corner leads to a
hollow flake traverse left to a terrifying,
but well-protected arête. At first glance
the arête looks like 5.10, but it's mercifully
covered with good incut holds and cracks.
Don't hesitate to use the "beached whale"
technique" when pulling onto the belay
ledge. Save 1-3" cams for the belay.

The third pitch starts with one of Lover's
Leap's few mandatory chimneys followed
by an exposed face traverse to the corner.
Fifty feet of stemming and jamming then
dike-hiking to the rim. A more sparsely
protected 5.8 variation goes straight up
from the wide crack instead of traversing
right to the corner

G. Power Lust   5.11a★★★★

FA: unknown

Evenly spaced small dikes on a near-vertical
wall. Height-dependent; harder than 5.11a
for shorter folks. Easy to toprope after
climbing Blue Cab.

H. Blue Cab   5.9★★★

FA: Blue Blocker, Taxi Dave, 7/03.

Dike climbing around a crack with
occasional jams. Sustained. From the
anchors, you can rap over and toprope
Power Lust. Great option if Corrugation
Corner is too crowded. Rappel with two
ropes or one 70m rope.

North Face, Pitch 1 (not shown)   5.7★★★

FA: Ken Edsburg, Jay Davidson, 1963.
FFA: M. Andrews, J. Orey, 1979.

This is a four-pitch route but only the
first 5.7 pitch is described here. It's a
good option if Corrugation Corner is too
crowded. Start 10 feet left of Stem Meister
and follow a shallow left-facing corner
with some of the biggest dikes at The Leap.
When the corner peters out, follow broken
face and small ledges to a major ledge in a
giant white alcove. Belay off an old piton
and bolt. Descend by traversing 15 feet left
to the Blue Cab anchors and rappelling 115
feet to the ground.
Rack: cams: 1-2 ea .4-3.5"

I. Stem Meister   5.10a★★★

FA: John Robinson, Will Cottrell, 1998.

Fun and sustained stemming corner that is
steeper than it looks.

J. Yankee Dog   5.11c★★★

FA: Mark Nicholas, 1996.

Bouldery dike moves to broken cracks. Can
toprope after climbing Stem Meister by
making 5.10 move right.

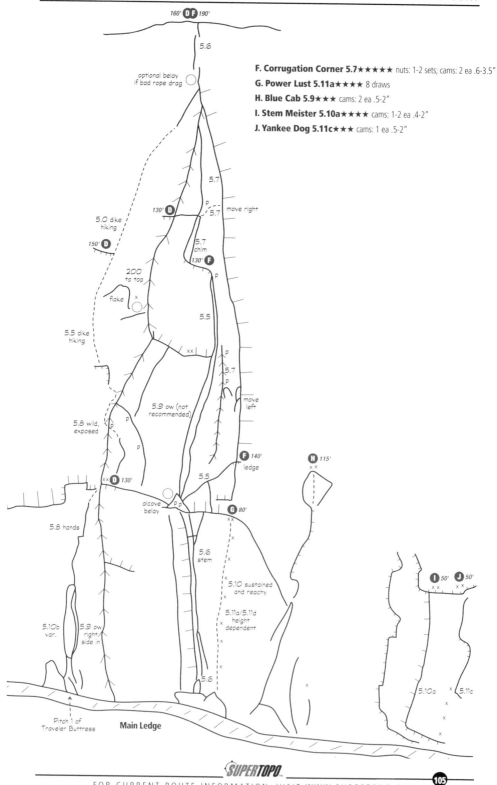

F. Corrugation Corner 5.7★★★★★ nuts: 1-2 sets; cams: 2 ea .6-3.5"
G. Power Lust 5.11a★★★★ 8 draws
H. Blue Cab 5.9★★★ cams: 2 ea .5-2"
I. Stem Meister 5.10a★★★★ cams: 1-2 ea .4-2"
J. Yankee Dog 5.11c★★★ cams: 1 ea .5-2"

WEST WALL

K. Arctic Breeze　　　　　　　5.10a★★★★

FA: Mike Carville, Lon Harter, 1995.

Exciting steep face lead recommended for confident 5.10a leaders. Immediately place a few pieces for belayer. After, consider toproping a dirty 5.10a variation to the left and Nirvana to the right. Can only toprope with 70m rope.

L. Nirvana　　　　　　　　　　5.11c★★★★★

FA: Jay Smith, 1993.

Incredible arête moves; incredible position. Bolts right at cruxes, then a tiny bit runout on easier terrain. Optional small cams and medium nuts for second pitch. Link both pitches to attain true enlightenment. Climb with one 70m rope or carry a second rope to rappel.

M. Hospital Corner　　　　　　5.10a★★★★★

FA: unknown; FFA: Richard Harrison, Jay Smith, 1977.

The best 5.10a at Lover's Leap. The first pitch is good but the exquisite steep second pitch corner defines the route. The crux pitch drains you with consistently steep and powerful hand jams and lieback moves. Good stemming technique is critical to keep your forearms from exploding. Conserve energy down low as the route gets harder up high. Either bring one 70m rope or two 50m ropes to rappel this climb.

N. The Gamoke　　　　　　　　5.10b★★★

FA: Richard Harrison, Jay Smith, 1977.

First pitch wanders a little. Second pitch features steep and incredible stemming and jams. A step up in difficulty from Hospital Corner.

O. Anesthesia　　　　　　　　5.11c★★★

FA: Troy Carliss, John Scott, and friends.

Most climbers do just the first pitch. Some mediocre gear placements to the first bolt then sustained 5.8 face. We do not show the second and third 5.11 pitches. Toprope the second pitch by rappelling from the top of Hospital Corner.

P. Main Line　　　　　　　　　5.11c★★★

FA: Jay Smith, Bill Todd, 1976.
FFA: John Bachar, Ron Kauk, 1978.

Another drug-theme named climb from the 1980s. Usually toproped after climbing Magnum Force.

Q. Magnum Force　　　　　　　5.10b★★★

FA: Greg Dexter, Jay Smith, 1977.

Spicy crux start protected by micro cams—careful! Then sustained, sharp, fingerlocks to a step left to anchors. A hard and heads-up 5.10b. Good linkup with Hospital Corner.

K. Arctic Breeze 5.10a★★★★ 8 draws

L. Nirvana 5.11c★★★★★ nuts: 1 set; cams: 1 ea .4-5"; 8 draws

M. Hospital Corner 5.10a★★★★★ nuts: 1 set; cams: 2 ea .5-3"

N. The Gamoke 5.10b★★★★ cams: 2 ea .5-3"

O. Anesthesia 5.11c★★★ nuts: 1 set; cams: 1 ea .5-1"; 6 draws

P. Main Line 5.11c★★★★ cams: 2 ea .4-2", 1 ea 3-4.5"

Q. Magnum Force 5.10b★★★★ cams: 2 ea .4-2"

MN 110'
X X

5.10a
stem/
hands

50' L
X X
X

5.10b
steep
stemming
hands

sustained
5.9

110' L X
X X

M 110'
X X

10b
N 120'

110' K X X

100' O X X

5.8

5.8

10a
var.

10a

5.8 5.9 step
right

5.8

hollow
flakes

11c

M

N Main Ledge

approach

to
Corrugation
Corner

80' PQ belay takes
.6-1.5'

5.11c
thin
hands

5.12

reach left

5.10b

3-
4.5'

sustained
5.10a

open
project

mantel

10b

200 feet to
Tombstone Ledge

P Q

Dear John Buttress

Approach time: **15-20 minutes**

Sun exposure: **partial morning**

Height of routes: **30–80'**

Chris McNamara

This cliff features challenging cracks on a steep, gorgeous, lichen-stained wall. Full afternoon shade makes it a great place to escape the heat and the wall is so steep that it's one of the few Tahoe cliffs that's dry in the rain.

Most climbs are short but steep enough to get you pumped—especially if you do laps. The excellent extensions to most climbs are hard and rarely climbed.

Toprope

It's common to climb the 5.9 corner variation to God of Thunder, then toprope the two cracks to the right. It's possible to traverse right and toprope the right cracks. Once warmed up, lead Rehab. This area is dusty, so bring a large rope bag.

Approach

Dear John lies a few hundred feet up and to the right of the Lower Buttress. Fifty feet east of the campground bathrooms, pick up the Old Pony Express Trail and walk a few hundred yards. When nearly perpendicular to the Lower Buttress on the right, turn right onto a climbers' trail and walk another 100 yards to the base. Turn right and follow switchbacks up the steep hill. When almost even with the top of Lower Buttress, veer right on a climbers' trail and walk a few hundred feet up and right to Dear John Buttress.

Descent

Rappel most climbs with one 60m rope.

A. Stony End   5.11c★★

FA: Tony Yaniro, Max Jones, 1982.

The lower arête is relatively unprotected 5.10a. The upper arête is 5.11c. Rarely led.

B. Drug Crazed   5.11c★★

FA: Tony Yaniro, Max Jones, 1984.

On the first pitch, climb steep and powerful fingerlocks left of the arête. Grovel left to bolts. Can toprope if you do a 5.10a hand traverse down from God of Thunder and Stone Cold Crazy anchors. Need a 1" piece as a directional.

C. Stone Cold Crazy   5.12c★★★★

FA: Tony Yaniro, 1982.

Start in the hand crack and traverse right to thin flaring crack. Punch up crack, milking the few real jams. Extremely bold lead on dicey gear. First lead without pre-placed gear by Paul Crawford.

D. Fight the Power   5.12b/c★★★★★

FA: Mike Carville, Dave Hatchett, 1990.

Maybe the best 5.12 at the Leap. Incredible crack climbing to incredible face climbing. Technical and pumpy. Big air potential on lead. To set a toprope, walk to the top of the cliff and rappel in.

E. God of Thunder   5.11c★★★★

FA: Dario Gambetta, Tony Yaniro, 1978.

Many cracks and variations. On the first pitch of the standard right start, climb a thin crack and make a balancy and reachy step right. Hand jams lead to a 5.11a finger lock/reach crux. Take a few laps.

The second pitch is rarely climbed. Steep 5.9 hands and face up to a 5.11b fist and lieback roof to a 5.9 offwidth. Then a final 5-foot roof (reach for the rail). A big reach to a small dike gets you over the anchors.

5.10c crack variation★★★
Strenuous jamming with rests. Well-protected. Stay right of the corner.

5.9 corner variation★★★
Fun stemming and jamming. Most climbers lead this pitch, then toprope the cracks to the right.

Tag Team (not shown)   5.10a★★

FA: Petch Pietrolungo, Brent Kimerly.

Start with the 5.10 variation of Gods of Thunder and continue past anchors in left crack. Next, make a 5.10 traverse left under a big ceiling and link up with Rehab. When moving past the ceiling, the rope has a tendency to get jammed.

F. Hushed Passage   5.10c★★

FA: Dave Schultz, 1996.

5.10c bolted arête, then step right to anchor or continue up to Rehab anchor. Set a directional for follower.

G. Rehab   5.11a★★★★

FA: Petch Pietrolungo, Brent Kuemerle.

Incredible mixture of steep crack and face. May want a thin nut or cam between second and third bolt. Another little crux above fourth bolt, then slightly overhanging 5.9 jamming to two-bolt anchor.

H. Sea Slug   5.11a★★

FA: Dan Kennedy.

Tricky gear placements at the flared crack crux where you jam, crimp, and stem.

I. Gods of Plunder   5.8★★

FA: unknown

A little dirty and adventurous. Face moves, then crack to a chimney. Move past chockstone to the top. Difficult to set a bomber toprope anchor.

J. Brother of John   5.8★★★

FA: unknown

Face moves lead to somewhat dirty flared cracks. Difficult to set a bomber toprope anchor.

K. Skism   5.11c★★

FA: Mark Nicholas, 1996.

Tricky face to arête. A little cruxy getting to the first bolt. Optional gear placement above the crux. From the same anchor you can toprope a 5.10c crack through a roof that then diagonals up and right.

Chris McNamara

A. Stony End 5.11c★★ cams: 1 ea .5-3.5"

B. Drug Crazed 5.11c★★★ cams: 1 ea .4-2"

C. Stone Cold Crazy 5.12c★★★★ tiny brass nuts; nuts; cams: 1 ea .4-1"

D. Fight the Power 5.12b/c★★★★★ cams: 1 ea .5-2.5"; 4 draws

E. God of Thunder 5.11c★★★★ Pitch 1: cams: 1 ea .5-2.5";
Pitch 2: cams: 1-2 ea .4-3", 2 ea 3.5-4.5", 1 ea 7"

F. Hushed Passage 5.10c★★ 3 draws

G. Rehab 5.11a★★★★ cams: 1 ea .5-3.5"; 3 draws

H. Sea Slug 5.11a★★ cams: 1-2 ea .4-2.5"

I. Gods of Plunder 5.8★★ cams: 1-2 ea .5-3.5"

J. Brother of John 5.8★★★ cams: 1-2 ea .5-4.5"

K. Skism 5.11c★★ 5 draws

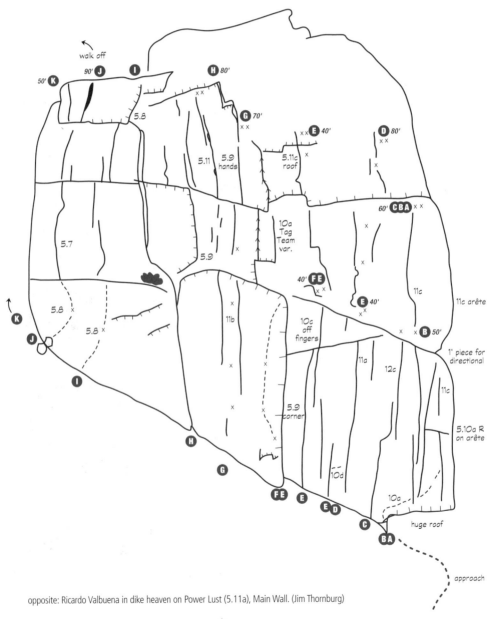

opposite: Ricardo Valbuena in dike heaven on Power Lust (5.11a), Main Wall. (Jim Thornburg)

Lower Buttress

Approach time: 5 minutes

Sun exposure: noon to afternoon

Height of routes: 200–350'

Lower Buttress is the most convenient Leap crag. It offers moderate multi-pitch routes, single-pitch 5.12 bolted climbs, and everything in between. Spend the whole day here or visit briefly if you're strapped for time and want a quick pump. This is a great warm-up for the Main Wall.

Approach

Fifty feet east of the campground bathrooms, find the Old Pony Express Trail and walk a few hundred yards. When nearly perpendicular to the Lower Buttress on the right, turn right onto a climbers' trail and walk another 100 yards to the base.

Descent

It takes 2-5 minutes to hike from the summit to the base. From the top, walk southwest, staying 50 feet from the edge.

Locate a climbers' trail that switchbacks down to the base.

A. Beer Can Direct 5.11a★★★

FA: unknown

Super sustained technical face climbing. A little sporty between bolts low and well-bolted up high. Can toprope with a 60m rope.

B. A Boy and his Arête 5.11a★★★

FA: Eric Gable, Petch Pietrolungo, 1996.

Not just a climb… an adventure. Not quite runout but you should be a solid 5.11 leader. Use long slings on all gear placements. Finish with a wild traverse above a roof (stay lower than you think). Carry a second rope to rappel.

C. Strawbilly Tango 5.12b★★★

FA: Petch Pietrolungo, Tad Steele, 5/01.

5.10a runout to first bolt. Super thin gastons and crimps past first and second bolts. A distance from last bolt to anchor on hard 5.11 (have belayer give slack so you don't crash into the roof).

Chris McNamara

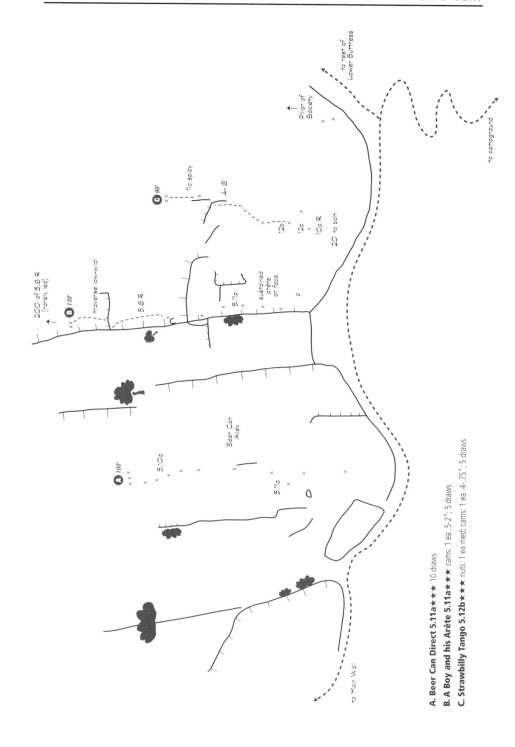

A. **Beer Can Direct 5.11a** ★★★★ 10 draws

B. **A Boy and his Aréte 5.11a** ★★ cams: 1 ea .5-2"; 5 draws

C. **Strawbilly Tango 5.12b** ★★★ nuts: 1 ea med; cams: 1 ea .4-.75"; 5 draws

D. Pillar of Society   5.12a★★★★

FA: Chris Clifford, Chris Pittman, 1984.

One of the best 5.12 face climbs at The
Leap. Bouldery start, then sustained for the
next four bolts. 5.10 and 5.11 to anchor.
Can set a toprope by traversing 30 feet on
5.4 R left from Surrealistic Pillar Direct
anchor.

E. Surrealistic Pillar   5.7★★★★★

FA: Ken and Mike Edsburg, Jerry Sublette, 1963.

While Surrealistic Pillar follows some large
cracks, it's almost entirely a face climb.
Recommended for solid 5.8 leaders because
while the harder moves are well-protected,
the easier climbing is runout.

   All of the few variations on the first pitch
climb steep and sustained dikes and cracks.
Keep the follower in mind when placing
protection on the first 40 feet. Belay at a
horizontal crack with 1-3" cams.

   For the second pitch, an unintuitive step
left leads to exposed 5.7 dikes and flakes.
Alternatively, go directly up the harder
5.8 arching corner, which protects with 7"
cams. Where the left-arching corner moves
back right, set gear and traverse left around
the arête—great exposure! A 50-foot 5.5
runout leads to a crack and then a belay
ledge.

   The last pitch climbs more runout 5.5
face. The second and third pitches barely
link with a 60m rope (note that you can't
hear your belayer).

F. 5.8 Variation

This variation has poor pro, poor rock and
is not recommended. On the second pitch,
instead of the dike traverse left around the
arête, trend right up cracks and belay 10
feet before a decomposing ledge. (Don't
belay on the ledge!) The last pitch climbs
decomposing, poorly protected cracks in a
corner or runout face on the right.

G. Surrealistic Pillar Direct   5.10b★★★★

FA: Jeff Low, Jean Vives III, 4/69.

A direct start to Surrealistic Pillar or a great
one-pitch climb in its own right. Easy to
toprope after climbing the first half of the
first pitch of Surrealistic Pillar. Entirely stem
or entirely jam the first 50 feet. There are
at least three 5.10a-5.10b finishes. Great
for doing laps on toprope and building
endurance.

H. 5.10b Variation

FA: Kurt Edsburg, et al, early 1960s.

This powerful hand-jamming test
culminates with 30 feet of steep and
relentless straight-in cracks. The initial 5.7
runout is sort of protected with a knob
tie-off. Place gear under the first roof and
then move out left onto thin cracks. Now
the business: pull through the roof with
powerful hand jams. Once over the roof, the
crack is pumpy to the anchor with only a
few dike stances for forearm relief.

I. For Real Crack   5.8★★★

FA: Gene Drake, M. Haymond, Jim Hicks, 1971.

Some jamming, squeezing, and liebacking.
But not as wide as it looks from the ground
as you often climb around the wide crack
on good holds.

J. Sinbad-Herbert   5.10d★★★

FA: Petch Pietrolungo, Blue Blocker, 2003.

Amazing overhanging hand crack and
stemming for 60 feet and then 130 feet of
great dike climbing. Use slings to reduce
rope drag. You can climb this route in two
pitches but it's better to climb one glorious
190-foot pitch. Because the pitch is so long,
use slings to manage rope drag. You get
bolts at the hard moves and bolts every
10-15 feet on the easier terrain. A final 5.6
R pitch to the top is not recommended.
Rappel to descend with two 60m ropes or
traverse right to The Groove bolt anchor.
Rappel from there with one 60m rope or
continue to the top.

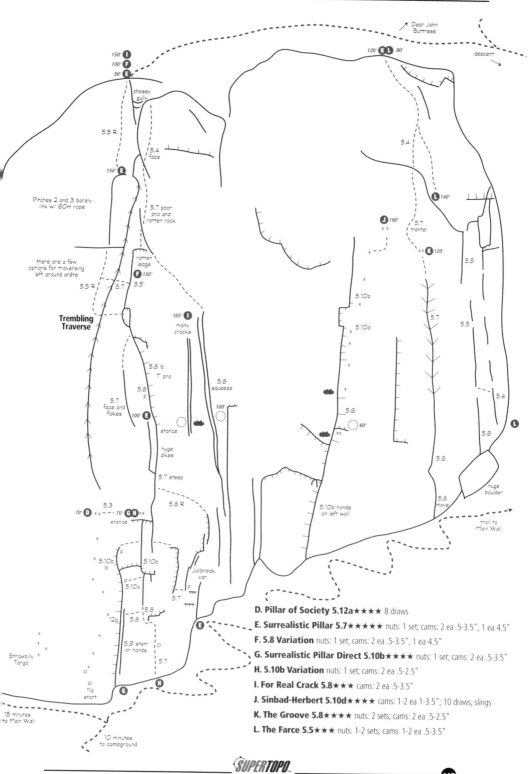

Dear John Buttress

descent

150' **I**
100' **F**
50' **E**

120' **K L** 90'

chossy gully

5.5 R

5.4 face

5.4

5.7 poor pro and rotten rock

5.4

150' **E**

L 140'

Pitches 2 and 3 barely link w/ 60m rope

J 190'
x x

5.7 mantel

rotten ledge

x x x **K** 120'

5.5

there are a few options for traversing left around arête

F 150'
5.7 3.5'

5.5 R

5.10b
x

5.7

5.5

Trembling Traverse

165' **I**
many cracks

5.10d
x

5.8 lb
7 pro

5.8 squeeze

x

5.8
P

100'

5.4

5.7 face and flakes

100' **E**

stance

5.6

60'

huge dikes

5.7 steep

5.8 R

5.6

huge boulder

5.3

5.10b hands on left wall

5.8 move

trail to Main Wall

70' **D** x x 70' **G H** x x
stance

x

L

x 5.10b lb

5.10b

P

5.10a

Jailbreak var.

5.7

P

5.8

12a 5.8

5.9 stem or hands

5.7

Strawbilly Tango

x
o

11d start

G

M

E

15 minutes to Main Wall

10 minutes to campground

D. Pillar of Society 5.12a★★★★ 8 draws

E. Surrealistic Pillar 5.7★★★★★ nuts: 1 set; cams: 2 ea .5-3.5", 1 ea 4.5"

F. 5.8 Variation nuts: 1 set; cams: 2 ea .5-3.5", 1 ea 4.5"

G. Surrealistic Pillar Direct 5.10b★★★★ nuts: 1 set; cams: 2 ea .5-3.5"

H. 5.10b Variation nuts: 1 set; cams: 2 ea .5-2.5"

I. For Real Crack 5.8★★★ cams: 2 ea .5-3.5"

J. Sinbad-Herbert 5.10d★★★★ cams: 1-2 ea 1-3.5"; 10 draws; slings

K. The Groove 5.8★★★★ nuts: 2 sets; cams: 2 ea .5-2.5"

L. The Farce 5.5★★★ nuts: 1-2 sets; cams: 1-2 ea .5-3.5"

K. The Groove 5.8★★★★

FA: unknown. FFA: Richard Harrison, Jay Smith, 1977.

Imagine climbing a 6-foot diameter water pipe that has been cut in half—that's The Groove. Large dikes, liebacking, and stemming on a near vertical wall. The first move 5.8 crux leads to sustained 5.7. The second pitch starts with tricky routefinding and a 10-foot runout to a heady 5.7 mantel. The difficulties then ease. With a 60m rope, you can rappel to the ground from the first anchor.

L. The Farce 5.5★★★

FA: unknown

A great introduction to The Leap and one of the steeper 5.5s you will ever climb. However, you should be a 5.6 leader as routefinding is tricky and many climbers inadvertently do 5.6 and even 5.7 moves. Follows a network of large crack systems that you often stem around on large dikes. Climb the route in two 100-foot pitches or one long 60m pitch.

M. Hemroids in Flight 5.10c★★★

FA: Rick Cashner, Darrell Hatten, Rick Sumner, 1979.

Start left on the face, climb up, clip first bolt, then move back right. 5.10 flared jams at second bolt then powerful roof crux. Step left and run up easy climbing then move back right under roof for anchor.

N. Voodoo 5.12d★★★★

FA: Petch Pietrolungo, 2002.

Thin slab start to 15 feet of unrelenting and powerful 5.12 through a bulge. One of the hardest climbs at The Leap. After crux, step right and finish Black Pyre. Can toprope with 70m rope.

Toprope Beta

Toprope the next four climbs with a 60m rope from a single gear anchor below the last bulge to the summit. Use a cordalette to equalize the anchor and extend it 15 feet with slings to reduce rope drag. An efficient way to get a lot of climbing in.

O. Black Pyre 5.11a★★★

FA: Paul Crawford, Jay Smith, 1980.

Awesome steep finger jams through bulge, then slab climbing to top. Surprisingly positive jams in a flared crack.

P. Black Opal 5.10c★★★

FA: Paul Crawford, Jay Smith, 1980.

Pumpy flared cracks with a humbling bulge to lower angle climbing. Start using both cracks. In the middle of the crux bulge, trend right.

Q. Black Magic 5.11c★★

FA: Paul Crawford, Jay Smith, 1980.

Start using both cracks and then move right when possible. Usually toproped.

R. Blue Wind 5.10a★★★

FA: Jay Smith, Rick Sumner, 1976.

Last crack you encounter on the Lower Buttress. Steep, awkward fingers and hands lead to strenuous off hands and lieback. Finish with lower angle wide cracks and face.

M. Hemroids In Flight 5.10c★★★ cams: 1 ea .6-3"; 3 draws
N. Voodoo 5.12d★★★★ cams: 1 ea .5-2"; 3 draws
O. Black Pyre 5.11a★★★ cams: 1-2 ea .5-2"
P. Black Opal 5.10c★★★ cams: 1-2 ea .5-2"
Q. Black Magic 5.11c★★ cams: 1-2 ea .5-2"
R. Blue Wind 5.10a★★★ cams: 2 ea .4-4"

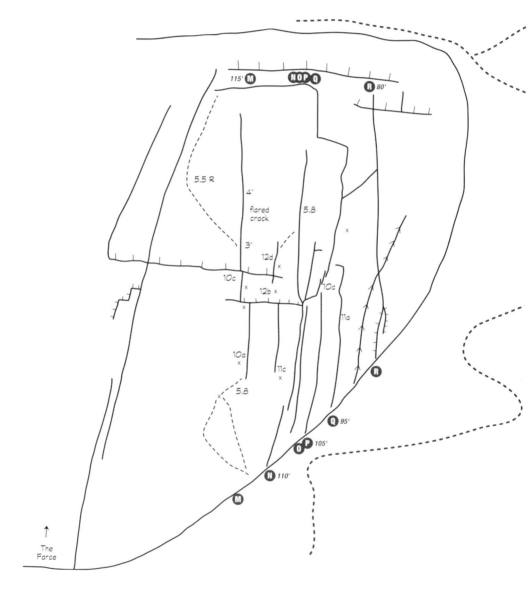

Hogwild

Approach time: **5 minutes**

Sun exposure: **noon to afternoon**

Height of routes: **80–120'**

Hogwild is one of the most accessible parts of Lover's Leap and has fewer crowds than the East Wall. Just five minutes from the campground, it offers a number of fun climbs, mostly one pitch and in the 5.7-5.10a range. It receives intense afternoon sun, so climb here on cool spring and fall days or summer mornings.

Approach

From the northwest end of the parking lot walk north under the telephone poles. After about 100 yards, at pole number 2569, turn right and follow a climbers' trail for a few hundred yards until you see the cliff at right.

Descent

Descend most routes by rappelling with one 60m rope. The only climb with a walk off is "It's Better With Bacon."

A. Accessory Dogs 5.10a★★★★

High quality face is sporty but not runout. Sometimes hard to find the easiest passage.

B. Unknown 5.8 R★★

Wandering and runout face moves. Rarely led but definitely worth toproping after climbing Accessory Dogs.

C. Just Acquaintances 5.6★★

FA: Tad Steele, Linda Jarret.

Follow the obvious crack in the center of the buttress. Its best to top out and walk down and around which is kinda a pain, or you can rap off a tree to accessory dogs and then back to the ground with one rope.

D. Soggy Biscuit 5.9★★

5.9 Variation to Just Acquaintances. Up main system, then traverse left above bulge.

E. Mixologist 5.9★★

FA: Petch Pietrolungo.

Follow overlaps to a bulge, bolt and the 5.9 crux, to a thin crack which widens to 4 inches. The 5.9 Bar Maid variation is at left.

F. Hogwild   5.7★★★★

Maybe the best single 5.7 pitch at The Leap.
Starts with a mixture of bolts and crack for
protection then just crack. Sustained 5.7
moves. Can toprope and descend with a
70m rope (otherwise you must carry two
ropes).

G. No Gaynor   5.9★★★

Face climbing with a crack. Thin at crux.
From last piece of gear make a runout 5.5
traverse to Hogwild anchors to belay.

H. It's Better With Bacon   5.8★★★

FA: Petch Pietrolungo, Brent Kuemerle, Chris McNamara, 8/03.

Great intro to 5.8 multi-pitch climbing.
Large ledges give the illusion that the wall
is not as long and steep as it actually is.
The first pitch climbs cool seams that only
take tiny brass nuts and cams. If you're
not confident placing tiny pro, then climb
the 4th class to the right and toprope this
section.

The second and third pitches climb face
with bolts at the cruxes. At the second belay,
step left to the corner to reduce the pitch to
5.6 (this makes the entire route only 5.7).
The fourth pitch climbs the main corner
with a few tricky bulges and good gear. It's
easy to miss the bolted anchor on the left.

Most climbers rappel the entire route
from the fourth anchor with one 60m
rope. However, climb the dirty pitch to
the summit if you want a stunning view
of Lover's Leap. From there you have three
options: rappel with one 60m rope back to
the fourth anchor and down the route, hike
west down to the campground, or hike east
down broken 3rd and 4th class slabs back
to the base. Because the first ledge has many
loose rocks, manage the rope carefully and
don't knock rocks onto climbers below.

Chris McNamara

A. Accessory Dogs 5.10a★★★ cams: 1 ea .5-.75", 5 draws
B. Unknown 5.8 R★★ cams: 1 ea .4-3", 3 draws
C. Just Acquaintances 5.6★★ cams: 1-2 ea .5-3"
D. Soggy Biscuit 5.9★★

E. Mixologist 5.9★★ cams: .5-3"
F. Hogwild 5.7★★★★ cams: 1-2 ea .5-1.5", 3 draws
G. No Gaynor 5.9★★★★ cams: 1-2 ea .5-2"

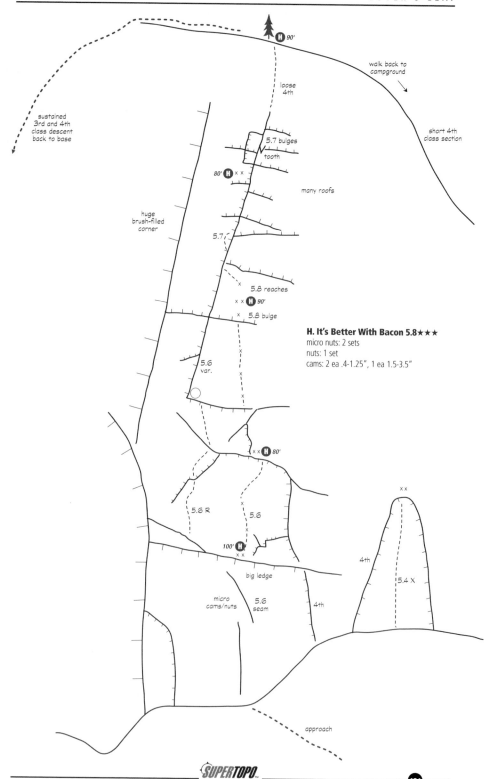

walk back to
campground

short 4th
class section

90'

loose
4th

sustained
3rd and 4th
class descent
back to base

5.7 bulges
tooth

80' H x x

many roofs

huge
brush-filled
corner

5.7

5.8 reaches
x x H 90'
x 5.8 bulge

H. It's Better With Bacon 5.8★★★
micro nuts: 2 sets
nuts: 1 set
cams: 2 ea .4-1.25", 1 ea 1.5-3.5"

5.6
var.

x x H 80'

x x
5.6 R
x
5.6
4th
5.4 X

100' H
x x

big ledge

micro
cams/nuts
5.6
seam
4th

approach

Hogsback

Approach time: 20 minutes

Sun exposure: noon to afternoon

Height of routes: 300'

The North Face of Hogsback is a great introduction to Lover's Leap and trad climbing in general. The 300-foot-wall is less steep, less dramatic and has smaller dikes than the rest of Lover's Leap. However, the climbs are fun and the lower-angle rock makes it less intimidating. There are enough routes for at least a full day of climbing. Advanced climbers should note that all the three-pitch climbs can be climbed in two pitches using intermediate belays and all the two pitch routes can be climbed in one 65m pitch (some simul-climbing required with 60m rope). Early in the climbing season, bring a nut tool to clean out the munge in some of the protection placements.

Approach

Pick up the Old Pony Express Trail 50 feet east of the campground bathrooms. When even with a notch in Hogsback's east should (and just after the Pony Express Trail turns right), turn left onto a climbers' trail that follows a subtle drainage path. Follow the switchbacks up for 100 yards through brush to the east shoulder of Hogsback. The trail then drops down and loops around to the southwest. Follow the trail for another few hundred yards to the base of the North Face.

Descent

From the top of Hogsback, walk down the east shoulder and join the approach trail. Walk back to the base. Most climbers carry comfortable descent shoes on the climb.

A. Knapsack Crack   5.5★★★

FA: unknown

This climb is great for first time Lover's Leap climbers. The route ascends 300 feet of clean, moderate, and well-protected terrain. Except for a few 5.5 moves around the second belay, the route is mostly 5.0-5.4 and is a perfect follow for a first time climber. Climb the route entirely as a face climb or use some of the cracks to practice jamming. The last two pitches link with one 60m rope.

B. Deception   5.6★★★

FA: Gene Drake, Larry Morris, 1969.

This is the most popular Hogsback climb. It delivers sustained and wandering 5.6 moves up the tallest part of the wall. The routefinding can be tricky so follow the topo closely. On the second pitch, the route climbs over some scary stacked blocks then makes a tricky 5.6 traverse left. For a harder variation, climb the splitter finger crack above the stacked blocks. High on the second pitch, a traverse right avoids the direct 5.7 variation. While it appears tame, the direct 5.7 variation does require some awkward moves on small gear. The route can be climbed in two pitches if you set the first anchor after climbing more than 150 feet.

Todd Offenbacher trying not to grease off It's Better With Bacon. (Chris McNamara)

C. Deception Direct   5.9★★★

FA: unknown

This route has 15 feet of scary 5.9 runout
face inserted in the middle of 300 feet
of moderate 5.6. The second pitch starts
modestly enough with fun 5.6 liebacking in
a big right-facing corner (bring extra 2.5-4"
cams to protect this well). The corner then
morphs into a tiny seam and the adventure
begins. Face moves, protected by RPs,
gradually get more difficult and culminate in
tenuous 5.9 face moves above questionable
gear. The rest of the climbing is 5.6.

D. Harvey's Wallbangers, Center   5.6★★

FA: unknown

The climb involves mostly 5.4 moves with
one short 5.6 fingers crux. This is a good
step up from Knapsack Crack and definitely
easier than Deception. Near the top, either
climb a 5.7 mantel or make an easy face
traverse right.

E. Harvey's Wallbangers, Right   5.7★★

FA: unknown

This climb is better and more sustained than
the Center route. Some of the first 30 feet of
dirty climbing can be avoided by climbing
on the right face. The pitch then ascends a
150-foot-long right facing corner with fun
liebacking, stemming, and the occasional
hand jam. If you set the first belay in the first
large pod, bring extra 2.5-3.5 cams. If you
set the belay 10 feet higher you have more
gear options. The awkward one-move 5.7
crux involves throwing your left hip into the
wide crack and liebacking the edge with your
right hand to get your body into a chimney
position. Protect the move with a 4.5" cam
or avoid the crux entirely by face climbing
left and joining the center route. A second
crux comes 10 feet higher on a 5.6 mantel
over a bulge that looks intimidating, but is
straightforward.

F. Manic Depressive Direct   5.5★★

Less sustained and less quality than
Knapsack Crack, this route is a great first
outdoor rock climb. The crux comes low
on face moves that protect with cams in
a pod in the flake. The route then climbs
the obvious diagonal crack to the summit
on mostly 5.4 and easier terrain. Note: the
original route (Manic Depressive) wanders
through the summit overhangs from the first
belay on runout 5.8 terrain.

G. Wave Rider   5.6 R★★★

FA: Gene Drake, Jim Hicks, 1970.

This is a great introduction to runout face
climbing. The moves are solid and the
protection, while sparse, offer some security.
The original right start is less direct with
more climbing, and has one bolt to protect
the first slab moves. To approach this start
you need to make an exposed 4th class
traverse from Harvey's Wallbangers or, skirt
the base of Hogsback around west until you
can make a 3rd class scramble up to the base
of the route. The direct start is unprotected,
but straightforward for the first 30 feet. From
the three-bolt first anchor, either move left
and join Manic Depressive or climb up and a
little right for 50 feet, then traverse back into
Manic Depressive for the last 10 feet. The
first pitch can be toproped with one 70m
rope or two 50m or 60m ropes tied together.
To set the toprope, climb Manic Depressive
for 130 feet and then step right to the bolted
anchor.

H. Unnamed   5.8 R★★

This climb is seldom led. The first 60 feet
are moderate and well-protected followed
by 5.7 slab moves that lead to a hole that
takes marginal gear. The face climbing turns
to pure friction involving as much faith as
technique. This climb can be toproped from
the bolted anchor if you tie two 60m or 50m
ropes together.

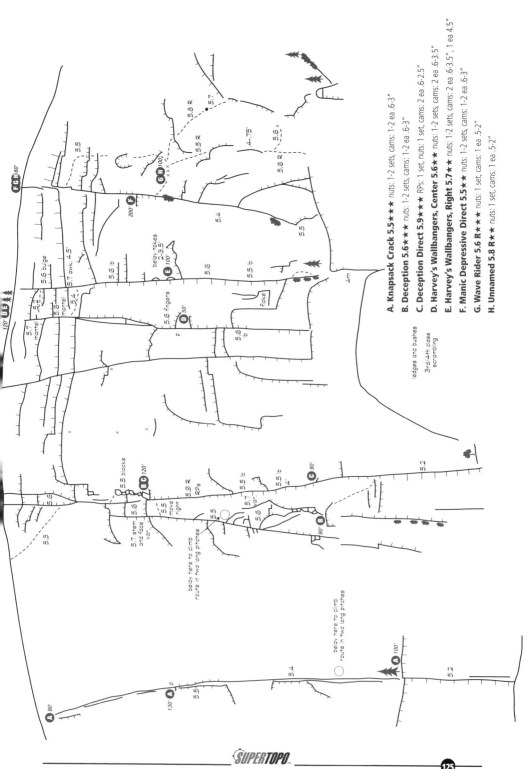

A. **Knapsack Crack 5.5★★** nuts: 1-2 sets, cams: 1-2 ea .6-3"

B. **Deception 5.6★★** nuts: 1-2 sets, cams: 1-2 ea .6-3"

C. **Deception Direct 5.9★★** RPs: 1 set, nuts: 1 set, cams: 2 ea .6-2.5"

D. **Harvey's Wallbangers, Center 5.6★★** nuts: 1-2 sets, cams: 2 ea .6-3.5"

E. **Harvey's Wallbangers, Right 5.7★★** nuts: 1-2 sets, cams: 2 ea .6-3.5", 1 ea 4.5"

F. **Manic Depressive Direct 5.5★★** nuts: 1-2 sets, cams: 1-2 ea .6-3"

G. **Wave Rider 5.6 R★★★** nuts: 1 set, cams: 1 ea .5-2"

H. **Unnamed 5.8 R★★** nuts: 1 set, cams: 1 ea .5-2"

The Box

Approach time: **15 minutes**

Sun exposure: **afternoon**

Height of routes: **60–85'**

Chris McNamara

The Box sits high on a cliff band west of Lover's Leap, and is a great way to escape the crowds and get pumped on high-quality 5.11s and 5.12s. It has ideal conditions on summer mornings or spring and fall afternoons. If you're feeling fit, get in the ring for "Six Rounds of Boxing": Start on Optischnauzer and climb all the routes to the right: a 5.11a, 5.11b, 5.11c, 5,11d and two 5.12bs.

Approach

From the southwest end of the campground, walk south and then west under the telephone poles. Before the fourth pole from the campsite (many rusted cans under the pole) turn left onto a climbers' trail. Ten minutes of steep switchbacks up the hill lead to the first cliffs. Continue up the climbers' trail and slightly right to an exposed ledge. Walk west to the climbs.

Descent

Rappel all routes to descend.

A. Optischnauzer   5.11a★★★

Dikes on a steep arête with a reachy crux above the fourth bolt. Bring a few nuts and/ or a small cam to protect between the first and second bolt, and extra long slings for the anchors. 60 feet tall.

B. Endless Plight   5.11b★★★★

A scary lead with tricky pro and insecure moves for the first 15 feet (zero slider nut useful). After a heroic roof, the climb eases to sustained 5.10b tight hands. Usually toproped after climbing Optischnauzer. 60 feet tall.

C. Dog Party   5.12b★★★★★

One of the best 5.12 cracks in Tahoe. Endurance stemming, lieback, and finger locks. Unrelenting for the first 40 feet. Can toprope after climbing Optischnauzer by traversing right. 60 feet tall.

D. Powerbox   5.12b★★★★

Unusually steep and powerful moves for The Leap. Optional gear around the first fixed pin. 70 feet tall.

E. Box Envy   5.11c★★★

Crux above first bolt then easy and runout face climbing to a wild 5.10c roof. Because of the tricky gear placements before the roof, some climbers move right and finish on Magic Box. 85 feet tall.

F. Magic Box   5.11d★★★

Powerful incut holds and slopers for the first three bolts, then easier climbing. 60 feet tall.

Petch Pietrolungo on Dog Party, one of Tahoe's finest 5.12 cracks. (Jim Thornburg)

Campground Boulders

Bring the crash pad to Lover's Leap? Yes. While limited in quantity, the Lover's Leap boulders are exceptional. The high quality of granite is extremely textured and offers a wide variety of handholds. Most problems are in the V1-V4 range and offer everything from steep crimps and slopers to long traverses and short cracks. There are enough problems for a full day of bouldering.

Because this is the first print bouldering guide to Lover's Leap, the ratings are probably a bit off. Please help me out by emailing your disagreements with the ratings to chris@supertopo.com. Also, if you know of names for any of these problems, email that, too.

Approach

Pick up the Old Pony Express Trail 50 feet east of the campground bathrooms and walk a few hundred feet.

Number of Problems by Difficulty

VB - 1
V0 - 5
V1 - 5
V2 - 3
V3 - 9
V4 - 4
V5 - 3
V6 - 2

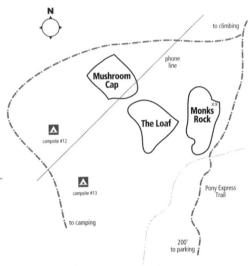

Sarah Felchlin traverses Monks Rock.

Chris McNamara

Monks Rock, Northeast Face (cave)

1. V4 – This 40-foot endurance test requires two or more spotters and as many crashpads. Start by hanging on the jug at the southeast corner of the overhang. Dyno with the right hand for a crimp, then bring the feet onto the slab. Easy traverse under the roof leads to the start of Problem 3. Do initial awkward jams on 3, but instead of finishing straight up, make a pumpy traverse right on giant holds with poor feet. Turn the corner and finish by traversing the (easier) northwest face.

2. V2 – This can be climbed as a boulder problem with a poor landing, or a toprope. To toprope, you will need at least 50 feet of rope and slings and biners for the two-bolt anchor (access the bolts via Problem 11. Start with thin hand jam(s), make a power and awkward move to a jug, then grunt over the bulge. Traverse left under a roof on awkward but easier moves.

3. V4 – Climb this as a boulder problem with a terrible, ankle-breaking landing, or a fun toprope. To set up the anchor, follow the instructions on Problem 2. Start on 2 but move right then straight up after pulling the first roof. The crux holds are not as positive as you would like.

Chris McNamara

Monks Rock, West Face

4. V3 – A sit start then powerful moves up a short steep section join up with the large shelf. Traverse right and finish on Problem 9 for a more difficult finish.

5. V0 – Fun traverse of northwest face across wild, colored rock.

Robbins Aid Ladder (not shown) – Rivets and bolts up the middle of the face.

Chris McNamara

Monks Rock, South Face

6. 5.7 – Chimney or stem up wide crack to top of boulder. (not shown)

7. V3 – Powerful slapping up the arête.

8. Unclimbed? – Horrendous slopers on a vertical wall.

9. V3 – Sit start to awkward arête-wrestling to a tough mantel.

10. V1 – Pockets to sidepull.

11. VB – This arête is the easiest path to the top of the boulder. From here, you can set a toprope off a two-bolt anchor for Problems 2 and 3.

Monks Rock, East Face (not shown)

12. (Left crack) V1 – Overhanging and awkward hands, fist, and lieback to high but easy face finish.

13. (Right crack) V0 – Overhanging bomber hand jams to high but easy face finish.

Chris McNamara

The Loaf, Northeast Face

14. V3 – An endurance test. Sit start backstepping right foot, then powerful move into a long hand traverse across the entire northeast face and around half of the northwest face. Finish whenever you feel like it.

15. V0 – Hand jam to mantel.

16. V0 – Lieback or fist jam.

17. V3 – Awkward lieback move to top.

18. V5 – Sit start to two-move wonder: awkward pinch followed by powerful pull to jug.

Chris McNamara

19. 5.12 offwidth – Do this and be worshipped. Sit down start. Boulder is off.

20. The easy way around the offwidth. Stand and jump to hold then lieback to top.

(Note: there are problems on the southwest side of the boulder, which generally have bad landings and mediocre climbing.)

Mushroom Cap, Northeast Face

21. V6 ? – Traverse across entire Northeast Face.

22. V4 ? – Desperate slab moves up black rock.

23. V3 – More desperate slab moves up black rock.

24. V5 – Good starting hold and tiny feet to thin and tricky moves to slab finish.

25. V6 – Thin and desperate to top.

26. V4 – Tricky traverse moves into Problem 28.

27. V5 – A hard starting move into Problem 28.

Chris McNamara

28. V3 – Most classic problem on the face. A tough start leads to a jug and then the business: grab slopers, get your feet up, and reach high. The finish is scary but manageable. Use many crash pads.

Chris McNamara

Mushroom Cap, Northwest Face (left)

29. V1 – Pinch dikes and slap arête. Awkward finish.

30. V0 – Start on horizontal crack then up dike to diagonal tips crack.

Mushroom Cap, Northwest Face (right)

31. V1 – Thin locks and side pulls with mediocre feet.

32. V1 – Powerful sidepulls.

Toprope Beta: You can toprope all climbs on this page by setting a gear anchor with a few 3-4" cams. Bring long slings to extend anchor.

Chris McNamara

Chris McNamara

Mushroom Cap, Southwest Face

33. V2 – Start just right of arête and use crack and the many facehold options.

34. V3 – Hard start to large sloper. Good fingerlock (bad feet), then big reach right. High finish on large incut holds.

35. V3 – Start in the right diagonal crack, then head straight up. Big reaches with small feet.

36. V2 – Hand traverse right then left.

Echo Lakes

Echo Lakes has all the quintessential Tahoe elements with expansive views of a lake, trees, and surrounding mountains. What is distinct about the area is the presence of many motor boats, which is a blessing and a curse. The available boat taxi offers a unique and convenient approach to the climbs. On the down side, the sound of boat engines infringes on an otherwise pristine outdoor setting.

Getting There

If driving west on Highway 50, coming from South Lake Tahoe, turn right on Echo Lakes Road (road sign hard to see) which comes 2.7 miles west of the junction of Highway 50 and Highway 89. Drive another 0.8 miles and trend right where the road forks. Drive another 0.6 miles and park in the paved or dirt parking lot. Walk down to the lake and the marina. Next, follow either the hiking or boat taxi information below.

If driving East on 50, take a left on Johnson Pass Road a few miles before Echo Summit (the road sign is hard to see). Drive 0.7 miles then take a left on Echo Lakes Road. Drive another 0.6 miles and park in the paved or dirt parking lot. Walk down to the lake and the marina. Next, follow either the hiking or boat taxi information below.

GPS Coordinate for the Cliff

38º 50' 778", 120º 04' 074"

Boat Taxi Info

Not enough time and money to enjoy the famous boat taxis in Thailand? Echo Lakes offers a similar experience at just a fraction of the cost… well, sort of. The boat taxi service opens at 7 a.m. and costs $7 per person ($4 for dogs) one way. Ask the driver to drop you off at the Mermaid Community Pier. To be picked up, you will either have to walk to the phone at the north end of the lake or use your cell phone to call the boat office (530-659-7207). Or, you can walk back 30 minutes on the trail.

When to Climb

Spring and fall have the best conditions. In the summer, the face gets intense sun and can be quite hot. If South Lake Tahoe temps are in the 80s then it's probably too hot to climb in the sun. In winter, the climbing would probably be warm in the sun but the approach is under snow.

Chris McNamara

Gangsta Wall

Approach time: **5 minutes (boat) or 30 minutes (hike)**

Sun exposure: **morning to late afternoon**

Height of routes: **80–200'**

Gangsta Wall is a sunny moderate crack and face climbing playground. It features a clean orange slab in the middle of a multi-tiered, low angle chunk of granite. The cracks are well-protected, making this a great place to learn to lead. The face routes are safely bolted but, in the tradition of slab climbing, they are usually more than a body length apart. You can climb most routes in a long 180+ foot pitch or in two 90-foot pitches. While not truly a "multi-pitch crag" this is a great place to practice your multi-pitch climbing skills. Most anchors are bolted.

The rock gets intense sun from morning to early afternoon. It may be too hot to climb here in the middle of the summer. Cool spring and fall days are perfect. Most climbers start on The Chronic or Thug Lite, then toprope climbs nearby.

The following rack works for most climbs: one 60m rope, 8 draws, 6 slings, cams 1 ea .5-3".

Toprope Beta

While it is difficult to walk to the top of the cliff to establish topropes, just about every anchor can be reached by climbing 5.6. One 60m rope is long enough to toprope most climbs.

Approach

This hike takes about 30 minutes and is relatively flat. From the marina, cross the outlet of Echo Lake and pick up the Pacific Crest Trail and hike along the north shore of the lake. After about 30 minutes, when you approach the northwest corner of the lake, look up and right to the big orange slab (this is the center of The Gangsta Wall). Gain the first tier and move up and right over a few hundred feet of 3rd class.

Descent

Descend all routes by rappelling once or twice with a 60m rope.

opposite: Chris Ewing topping out Thug Lite. (Chris McNamara)

Chris McNamara

A. Drive-by   5.10a★★★★

FA: Chris McNamara, Todd Offenbacher, Chris Ewing, 7/03.

Good mixture of face and crack climbing.
Bouldery arête move to mixed face and
crack. Second pitch starts with 5.8 hands
and moves to cool 5.9 face. Link both
pitches for 160 feet of cool climbing.

B. 2 of America's Most Wanted   5.8★★★

FA: unknown

Sustained 5.8 hands in corner. Often linked
with the second pitch of 5.10a.

C. Dr. and The Doberman   5.8 R★★

FA: Chris McNamara, 8/03.

Scary lead up cool seam or fun toprope
after climbing 5.8 corner.

D. The Chronic   5.8★★★

FA: Todd Offenbacher, Chris McNamara, 7/03.

Good warm-up climb. Slightly runout face
finish after third bolt or step right to crack.

E. California Love   5.9★★★★

FA: Todd Offenbacher, Chris McNamara, 7/03.

Almost a full 60m of incredibly sustained
and fun face climbing. Use many slings to
reduce rope drag.

F. Thug Life   5.8★★★

FA: unknown

Steep jamming at start then low-angle
slab. Long ways between bolts. Can stop at
anchor of 5.6 corner and toprope with 70m
rope or continue in one long pitch all the
way to top.

G. Thug Lite   5.6★★★

FA: unknown

Bouldery 5.6 moves at start and 5.6 lieback
up high. Can barely toprope with a 60m
rope. Second pitch is 5.1.

H. 12-Gauge Shotty   5.12a★★★

FA: unknown

A 5.11b face low to a 5.12a bulge up high.
Big fall potential at all cruxes. Toprope from
tree at top. Very sustained, bad bolts.

I. Bada-Bing!   5.10b★★★

FA: Chris McNamara, Chris Ewing, 7/03.

Wandering. Gear is not always right where
you want it. Tricky cruxes between cruiser
terrain. Anchor location makes it difficult to
communicate with follower.

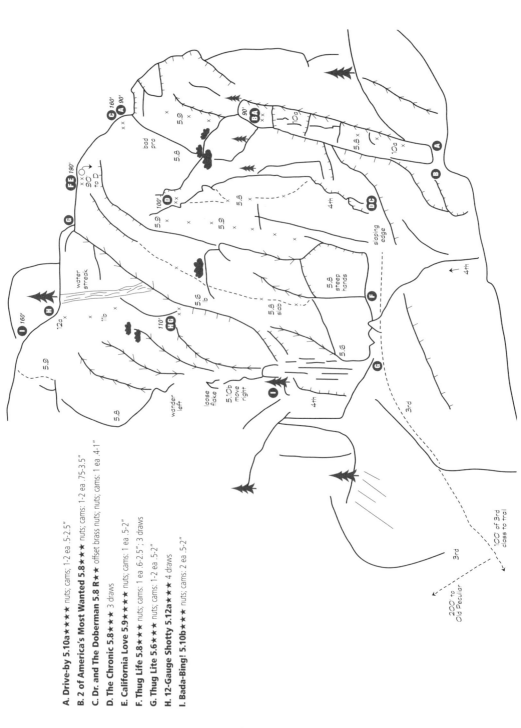

A. **Drive-by 5.10a** ★★★★ nuts; cams; 1-2 ea .5-2.5"
B. **2 of America's Most Wanted 5.8** ★★★ nuts; cams: 1-2 ea .75-3.5"
C. **Dr. and The Doberman 5.8 R** ★★ offset brass nuts; nuts; cams: 1 ea .4-1"
D. **The Chronic 5.8** ★★★ 3 draws
E. **California Love 5.9** ★★★★ nuts; cams: 1 ea .5-2"
F. **Thug Life 5.8** ★★★ nuts; cams: 1 ea .6-2.5"; 3 draws
G. **Thug Lite 5.6** ★★ nuts; cams: 1-2 ea .5-2"
H. **12-Gauge Shotty 5.12a** ★★★ 4 draws
I. **Bada-Bing! 5.10b** ★★★ nuts; cams: 2 ea .5-2"

Old Peculiar

Approach time: **10-30 minutes**

Sun exposure: **noon to sunset**

Height of routes: **30–50'**

This wall has steeper, harder, and shorter routes than the Gangsta Wall. There are some great 5.10 and 5.11 climbs and okay 5.9 and easier routes that can be toproped without too much hassle. Because the wall gets intense sun from noon on, it is great in the afternoon in cool months or early in the morning on warmer months. The rack for all climbs (and to establish toprope anchors) is: nuts; cams: 1-2 ea .5-3.5" plus some long slings to set anchors.

Toprope Beta

Toprope all climbs by walking up the left side of the cliff for a few hundred feet then traversing down and right to the anchors.

Approach

Old Peculiar is only a few hundred feet past the Gangsta Wall area. Follow the Gangsta Wall approach, then scramble left (northwest) a few hundred feet.

Descent

Descend all routes by traversing up and left until you reach a gully and can return to the base.

A. The Drill Press   5.12b★★★

FA: Dave Hatchett.

Many small roofs on steep and pumpy rock. Small gear between the second and third bolts. Can set a toprope by rappelling from Peon anchor.

B. Peon   5.10b★★★

FA: Dave and Mike Hatchett.

Wider crack to thinner crack to face. All sizes. Cruxy-looking bulge at top.

C. Freon   5.11c★★★

FA: Al Swanson, Mike and Dave Hatchett.

Thin crack to face. Protected by bolt.

D. Knee On   5.10b★★★

FA: Al Swanson, Dave and Mike Hatchett.

Can toprope off .5-1" for anchor.

NOTE: The next three climbs all anchor off slung chockstones that should be backed up with natural gear.

E. Old Peculiar   5.8★★★

FA: Mike Corbett, Bill Serniuk, Charlene Serniuk, 1979.

A little dirty with slightly awkward finish.

F. Yodeler   5.9★★★

FA: Mike Corbett, Bill Serniuk, Charlene Serniuk, 1979.

The 5.8 thin crack left start is best. Awkward finishing moves.

G. Sayonara   5.7★★

FA: Mike Corbett, Bill Serniuk, Charlene Serniuk, 1979.

The easiest route but not one of the best.

H. Offwidth Their Heads   5.9★★

FA: Rick Cashner, Mike Corbett, 1979.

This wide crack can be toproped from the Sun and Steel anchor.

I. Sun and Steel   5.11c★★★

FA: Dave and Mike Hatchett, Rick Lovelace.

Fun, technical thin face.

J. Hanus Anus   5.11b★★

FA: Dave and Mike Hatchett, Rick Lovelace.

Awkward moves into stemming corner to step right to crack.

Chris McNamara

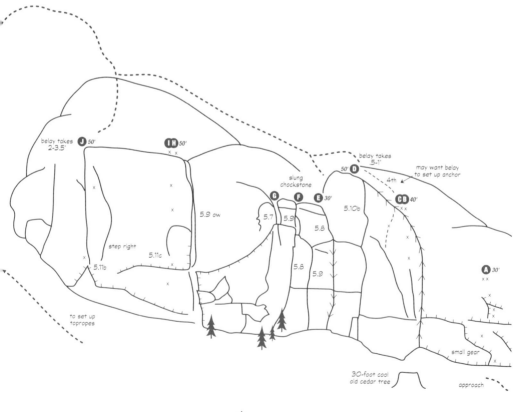

Berkeley Camp

Approach time: **2 minutes**

Sun exposure: **morning to noon**

Height of routes: **50'**

Two minutes east of Echo Lake, Berkeley Camp offers a small selection of convenient and quality 60-foot-tall sport climbs. The climbs sit a few hundred yards above Highway 50 (lots of traffic noise) and have an expansive view of Lake Tahoe, Cave Rock, and the peaks on the east shore. The climbing ranges from under vertical technical face to steep and powerful liebacking and underclings, all on great rock and well-protected with bolts. For gear, bring seven quickdraws, one rope, and a few slings for anchors. With only a few hours of time you can still get a good pump.

Toprope Beta

This an extremely convenient place to toprope because you can walk to the top of every climb.

Getting There

If driving west on Highway 50, coming from South Lake Tahoe, turn right on Echo Lakes Road (the road sign is hard to see), which intersects 2.7 miles west of the junction of Highway 50 and Highway 89. Drive another 0.8 miles and trend right where the road forks. Drive another 0.4 miles and park on a small dirt pullout on the right before the Berkeley-Echo Lake Camp sign.

If driving East on 50, take a left on Johnson Pass Road a few miles before Echo Summit (the road sign is hard to see). Drive 0.7 miles, then take a left on Echo Lakes Road. Drive another 0.4 miles and park on a small dirt pullout on the right before Berkeley Camp.

Approach

From the Berkeley Camp sign, walk down the driveway and to the right of the main building. After another few hundred feet you pass a basketball court on the left and drop down the steep hillside 50 feet to the climbs.

When to Climb

Because the wall gets sun for half the day, there is almost always one time of day with ideal temperatures. In the summer, climb in the afternoon when the wall goes into the shade. On colder spring or fall days, climb in the morning.

A. First Stage 5.9★★

FA: unknown

Good warm-up. Sometimes broken rock, sometimes smooth face. Toprope the next two climbs from this anchor.

B. New Jersey Turnpike 5.11b★★★★

FA: Jay Sell.

Powerful, steep bulge crux to lieback. Finish on last bolt of First Stage.

C. Flu 5.11d★★★★

FA: Jay Sell, Jason Totallman.

Steep, powerful liebacking. Finish on last bolt of First Stage.

D. Witch Doctor 5.12b★★★★

FA: Chuck Brown.

Technical, powerful climbing over roof.

E. Salt Water Flush 5.10c★★★★

FA: unknown

Thin face left of arête.

F. Lelfie 5.12a★★★

FA: unknown

Boulder problem on arête. Stick clip first bolt.

Chris McNamara

A. First Stage 5.9★★★ 5 draws

B. New Jersey Turnpike 5.11b★★★★ 6 draws

C. Flu 5.11d★★★★ 6 draws

D. Witch Doctor 5.12b★★★★ 7 draws

E. Salt Water Flush 5.10c★★★★ 5 draws

F. Lelfie 5.12a★★★ 3 draws

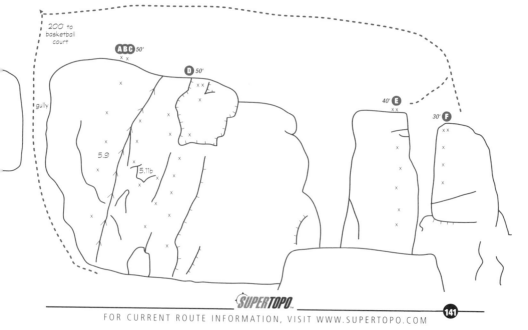

Luther Rock

Approach time: **30-40 minutes**

Sun exposure: **afternoon to sunset**

Height of routes: **60–100'**

Welcome to South Lake Tahoe's best 5.10-5.11 sport climbing. The granite is delightfully weird, with many edges, vertical eyebrows, and lichen streaks. The routes are vertical to slightly overhanging and concentrated. Instead of strenuous single crux moves often found on granite sport climbs, most of the routes here require endurance on good holds that don't stress your joints and are pretty easy on the fingertips. This is a great place to do a lot of pitches and get strong.

There are not many climbs you can walk to the top of and toprope. However, on half the climbs you can do an easier route, then swing over and toprope a harder route. The only rack you need is 10-14 quickdraws and a 60m rope.

Getting There

From the junction of Highway 89 and 50, drive 3.4 miles south on 89 and park in the third paved pullout on the right once you start up the grade. Climb the bank on the opposite side of the road and find the climbers' trail.

Approach

Avoid hiking in the sun on this strenuous approach. It takes 30-40 minutes, is 0.5 miles long, and gains 900 feet in elevation. The first two thirds ascend a steep climbers' trail. The last third goes up a fairly secure but steep scree gully. Once even with the cliff you are climbing (Detox Wall is the lower cliff and Distillery Wall is the upper cliff) then move right out of the scree gully.

When to Climb

The climbing starts when the snow melts off the approach (usually in May) and ends at the first winter storm (usually in early November). The routes face west and don't get sun until about 1 p.m. Climb here on hot summer mornings (start before the sun hits the approach) or cool spring or fall afternoons.

Chris McNamara

DISTILLERY WALL

A. Chip Shot   5.11b★★★

FA: Jay Sell, Brock Berry, 1996.

Climb a chimney to the first
bolt, then up the featured face.
Runout to first bolt. Not that
popular.

B. Moonshine   5.10c★★★★★

FA: Jay Sell, Brock Berry, Bob Schultz, 1996.

Luther Rock's best route.
Scramble up the 3rd class trail
along the base of the cliff to a
block. Climb to the top of the
block and start from there (the
direct start is 5.11a). The 5.10c
crux comes between first and
second bolt. A wide ledge 30
feet up provides a nice break
before the remaining 65 feet of
moderate, sustained, and truly
awesome climbing.

Chris McNamara

C. Seven and Seven   5.11c★★★★★

FA: Jay Sell, Brock Berry, 1996.

Technical crux low, then sustained,
overhanging, and pumpy crux up high.
Easy to toprope after climbing Moonshine
(clip many bolts for directionals).

D. Yards of Ale   5.11d★★★★

FA: Jay Sell, 1997.

Start on Bar Fly, then move left and join up
with Seven and Seven.

E. Bar Fly   5.11c★★★★

FA: Jeff Mayfield, Jay Sell, 1997.

Pumpy crux halfway through. A slabby,
reachy start leads to sustained hard
climbing with interesting fingerlocks
through the crux.

F. Five Nine   5.10a★★★

FA: unknown

Balancy moves up a thin face. Sustained.

G. After Hours   5.12a★★★

FA: Jeff Mayfield, Jay Sell, Brock Berry, 1997.

Traverse left at fourth bolt of Happy Hour
then pass the right side of the roof. The
short and steep crux comes above the roof.

H. Happy Hour   5.11b★★★★

FA: Steven Briggs, Brock Berry, 1997.

Start up a block. Step across to a secure
lieback, then up a featured corner.

Political Shots (not shown)   5.11a★

Scramble up a gully on the right side of
Distillery Wall. Climb bulgy, dirty, and
balancy face. Crux is clipping the anchors.
Rarely climbed.

Chris McNamara

DETOX WALL

I. Jonesin' 5.10a★★★★	**N. Straight Jacket** 5.11d★★★

FA: Jay Sell, Brock Berry, 1996.

FA: Steven Briggs, Brock Berry, 1997.

Don't be afraid of the blank looking face—great holds appear. Nice warm-up for the routes on the platform. One of the few routes where you can walk to the anchor and toprope.

Strenuous and sustained. Balancy start to an insecure crack, then up and around the corner. A small dyno awaits at the crux toward the top.

O. Intervention   5.10d★★★★

J. Methadone   5.10a★★★★

FA: Jay Sell, Brock Berry, 1996,

FA: Todd Offenbacher, Jay Sell, 9/00.

The leftmost route on the platform. Balancy bottom leads to featured face climbing.

Featured face climbing. Crux is at the third bolt over slabby holds through a balancy section.

K. With Draws   5.11a★★★★

P. Daily Prayer   5.10c★★★★

FA: Jay Sell, Brock Berry, 1996.

FA: Todd Offenbacher, Brad Jackson, 7/01.

Balancy start leads to a technical crux. Sustained.

Five bolts, then finish on last three bolts of Betty Ford's Route. Sustained climbing off the ground. Crux is pulling the roof, then the climbing eases. From anchor can toprope Intervention.

L. Loading Dose   5.11b★★★★

FA: Liz Wilson-Sell, Jay Sell, 1996.

Featured face climbing. Technical crux.

Q. Betty Ford's Route   5.9★★★★

M. Fallen Spirits   5.11c★★★★★

FA: Todd Offenbacher, Jack Sell, 7/00.

FA: Jay Sell, Brock Berry, 1996.

Great warm-up climb at the cliff. From anchor can toprope both Daily Prayer and Intervention. Reachy crux.

The best route on the platform. Several hand jams provide a necessary rest for the crux toward the top of the climb.

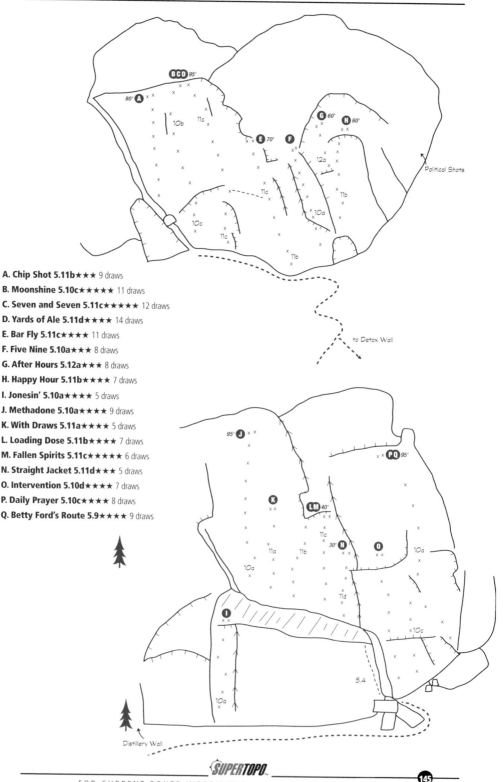

A. Chip Shot 5.11b★★★ 9 draws

B. Moonshine 5.10c★★★★★ 11 draws

C. Seven and Seven 5.11c★★★★★ 12 draws

D. Yards of Ale 5.11d★★★ 14 draws

E. Bar Fly 5.11c★★★ 11 draws

F. Five Nine 5.10a★★★ 8 draws

G. After Hours 5.12a★★★ 8 draws

H. Happy Hour 5.11b★★★★ 7 draws

I. Jonesin' 5.10a★★★★ 5 draws

J. Methadone 5.10a★★★★ 9 draws

K. With Draws 5.11a★★★★ 5 draws

L. Loading Dose 5.11b★★★ 7 draws

M. Fallen Spirits 5.11c★★★★★ 6 draws

N. Straight Jacket 5.11d★★★ 5 draws

O. Intervention 5.10d★★★★ 7 draws

P. Daily Prayer 5.10c★★★★ 8 draws

Q. Betty Ford's Route 5.9★★★★ 9 draws

Luther Spires

Chris McNamara

Luther Spires is a great introduction to Lake Tahoe sport climbing. The area has incredibly featured rock with big incut holds that are rare to find on granite. This area is located in the same general area as Luther Rock but has a completely different approach. The routes range in height from 25-60 feet and most are well-protected with bolts. A single 50m or 60m rope and eight quickdraws are enough for most climbs. A few pieces in the .6-1.25" are necessary on a couple of climbs. All anchors have two bolts and chains. Most people warm up on Jane Spy, Dog and Gri Gri, Two Bucks and Beer and Hot Dog, Two Bucks. Then they move left.

History

After studying the cliff over hundreds of drives to Kirkwood Ski Resort, Todd Offenbacher finally decided to check out the climbing possibilities in the spring of 2002. When he found numerous spires with highly featured rock, he knew he had come across a fun cragging area. Only one route, the Original Route, preceded his visit. This was established by Chick Spacal (Chaz), known for his appearances in several ski mags in the 80-90s. Offenbacher put up the rest of the routes with the help of Bugsy Offenbacher, Brad Jackson, Virginia DeRosa, Terry Lilienfield, Tara Offenbacher, and Dave Salazar. Since most Tahoe sport crags feature routes in the 5.10 and 5.11 range, Todd was psyched to find a place with easier terrain in such a spectacular location. Because of his efforts, this is one of the uncrowded crags in Tahoe and great for learning to lead both sport and trad.

Toprope Beta

With one 60m rope you can toprope all climbs. Most of the climbs must be led to establish a toprope. Sometimes you can climb an easier route, then move the anchor and toprope a harder route. The routes to which you can walk to and establish a toprope are: A, B, C, L, N, U, and V.

Getting There

The approach takes 20-30 minutes and gains a few hundred feet in elevation. The approach to Luther Spires is easier than Luther Rock, mostly because you drive farther up Luther Pass and therefore have to gain less elevation.

From the junction of Highway 89 and 50, drive south on 89 (well past Luther Rock parking) to Big Meadow Trailhead. Luther Spires parking is 0.4 miles past Big Meadow Trailhead on the left (north) side of the road. The parking area is marked with several large boulders (often a cairn on the boulders). Cross the small open clearing and follow cairns across Rim Trail to a huge natural tree bridge over creek. From here the trail is well established and marked with cairns.

When to Climb

The climbing starts when the snow melts off the approach (usually in May) and ends at the first winter storm (usually in early November). The routes face west and don't get sun until about 1 p.m. Climb here on hot summer mornings (start before the sun hits the approach) or cool spring or fall afternoons.

A. Beer and a Hot Dog, Two Bucks 5.8★★★

Climb a small spire with two ears on the top. The climb is short but fun on sustained and positive incut edges. 25 feet tall.
Rack: 4 draws

B. Dog and Gri Gri, Two Bucks 5.9★★

One 5.9 move as you pass the first bolt then turns to 5.7 on big incut holds. 30 feet tall.
Rack: 4 draws

C. Hey Y'all, Watch This 5.7★★

Thirty feet of mostly 5.5 crack climbing with a 5.7 move half way up.
Rack: nuts, cams: 1-2 ea to 2"

D. Jacko 5.10b★★★

Dead vertical. Tons of big holds to a distinct crux at the fourth bolt. 35 feet tall.
Rack: 5 draws

E. Just Jerry 5.9★★★

Really cool moves and great incut holds. 35 feet tall.
Rack: 4 draws

F. Jackass 5.11c★★★

5.11b crux low then can rest right. Steep and powerful. Gets shade in the morning, then the afternoon. Can toprope after climbing Jane Spy. 60 feet tall.
Rack: 6 draws

G. Jane Spy 5.7★★★★

The first lead for lots of people, but you should be a solid 5.7 climber because there is a fair distance between bolts and the rock is low angle enough that you don't want to fall. One of the most popular climbs at the cliff. Great warm-up. 60 feet tall.
Rack: 4 draws

H. Just Cause 5.10a★

Chimney start, then crux at fourth bolt. At one point you can step left to rest, which makes the route a little contrived. (Needs chains or quicklinks for anchor.) 50 feet tall.
Rack: 5 draws

I. See Thru 5.8★★

A great offwidth climb that takes gear in the features on both sides of the OW. Move left near the top to finish on Mixed Emotions' anchor.
Rack: nuts, cams 1-2 ea .5-3.5"

J. Mixed Emotions 5.10a★★★★

Striking line up a cool spire. Start with 35 feet of gear-protected crack to crux at third bolt. 70 feet tall.
Rack: nuts; cams: 1 ea .6-1.25"; 5 draws

K. Ringlock 5.10a★★★

Crux at fourth bolt. One of the better climbs. After you're done you can climb Mixed Emotions from the same anchor by carefully flipping the rope. 60 feet tall.
Rack: 7 draws

L. Guide's Route 5.7

Climb a low angle "buttress" and be the second accent. No one else will do it because this route is the only one NOT worth doing at the crag. Use Slab-B anchors to get down.
Rack: nuts, cams: 1 ea .5-2"

M. Slab-B   5.7★★

Cool slab climbing thru a roof. Good
second lead for beginner climbers after Jane
Spy 5.7.
Rack: 4 draws

N. Unnamed Toprope   5.10★

Thin moves to bigger holds.

O. Fire Starter   5.10c★★

Technical climbing on little holds. Thin
crux at second bolts, then mellows.
Optional .75 or 1" cam for the first 10 feet.
60 feet tall.
Rack: 6 draws

P. Plane Crash   5.10b★★★

Steep climbing on nice incut holds leads
to crux at fifth bolt. A plane crashed just
across the valley during the first ascent,
killing two people. The crash started a
large forest fire that closed Highway 88
for a day and threatened some homes in
the Christmas Valley. As Todd and friends
worked on the route, tanker planes dropped
their payloads on the fire: "The sky became
this wild yellow tint as the smoke made its
way to us and we were forced to leave by
choking smoke." Firefighters worked on this
fire for more than a week.
Rack: 7 draws

Q. Just Do It   5.10c★★★★

Crux at fourth bolt. Cruxes right off the
ground, then right above the fourth bolt. A
little runout above fourth bolt but you're on
big holds. 60 feet tall.
Rack: 7 draws

R. Virginia   5.10b★★★

This is an awesome finger-to-hand crack
climb with good feet and some jugs. Two
bolts have been added near the top after FA
to make this route safer.
Rack: nuts; cams: 1 ea .5-2"; 2 draws

S. Back Crack   5.9★

This is a short hand crack to top of Shire
Spire. From the top you can carefully move
to toprope anchors of the two other climbs
on the spire.
Rack: nuts; cams: 1 ea .5-2"

T. Original Route   5.11★★★★

This route is a classic and the first route to
be established at the crag. Steep hand jams
with good gear. Be ready to hang on!
Rack: nuts; cams: 1 ea .5-6", 2 ea .75-1.5",
1 ea 1.75-3"

U. Widow Maker   5.10a★★★

This is one of the best face climbs here. It
is easy and a little runout to first bolt. Then
climb well-protected, tricky thin moves to
the crux at the sixth bolt.
Rack: 7 draws

V. Undertaker   5.10b★★★

Climb up through cracks and broken flakes
to a finger crack that leads to a left-facing
ramp. Tricky move through the ramp to
a super cool steep finish on hidden jugs.
Mantel onto ledge, clip anchors.
Rack: nuts; cams: 1-2 ea .5-2"

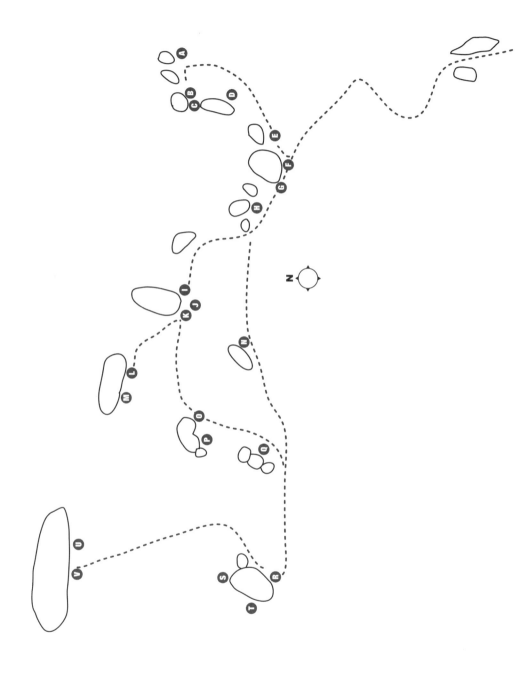

Eagle Creek Canyon

Chris McNamara

The expansive Eagle Creek Canyon has well over 15 established crags and many more awaiting discovery. The rock is all of high quality and varies between featured face and clean cracks. Climb sport routes near the road at Mayhem Cove or climb cracks in a wilderness area at Eagle Lake Cliff. The mouth of the canyon has great views of Lake Tahoe and the higher elevation areas have views of alpine lakes and surrounding peaks. This is one of the most popular Tahoe hiking trailheads and the parking lot and first mile of the trail can be a zoo. However, once you're at the cliffs, you generally escape the crowds. There is something for every ability, but most routes are in the 5.9-5.11 range. Most routes are convenient to toprope.

Getting There

Eagle Creek Canyon is located above Emerald Bay on the west shore of Lake Tahoe. If you're driving from the Bay Area, it's another 45 minutes past Lover's Leap. However, it's worth the extra drive if you are either looking for harder sport climbing or more Yosemite-style clean cracks.

From "The Y" at the west end of South Lake Tahoe, drive 9 miles (20 minutes) south on Highway 89/Emerald Bay Road and park at the Eagle Lakes Trailhead. Get free parking on Highway 89 or pull into the main parking area and pay $3. (Be warned that on weekends the parking usually fills up by the late morning).

When to Climb

Eagle Creek Canyon has a similar climbing season to Lover's Leap. You can climb here when the snow melts, usually in May, and climb here until the first snows come, usually in November. Some area of the canyon are always either in the sun or shade so it has ideal climbing conditions. On hot days, start climbing at Eagle Lake Cliff or Eagle Creek Wall in the morning and then move to 90-Foot Wall, Mayhem Cove, or Eagle's Nest in the afternoon.

For a weather forecast, check South Lake Tahoe: http://www.weather.com/weather/local/USCA1083

Camping

Camp Richardson, located halfway between Emerald Bay and South Lake Tahoe, offers the closest camping. Be advised that this is a huge campground. Each site costs $17-25 and sleeps six. For more info visit: http://www.camprich.com.

For free camping, go to Phantom Spires or Lover's Leap.

Cell Phones

There is spotty cell coverage at the parking area and on the approach. There is good coverage at Mayhem Cove. Most other climbing areas have poor coverage.

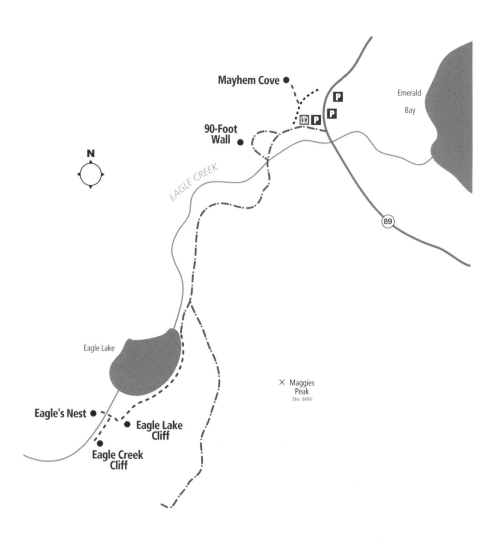

Mayhem Cove ●

Emerald
Bay

90-Foot
Wall ●

N

EAGLE CREEK

89

Eagle Lake

Eagle's Nest ●

Eagle Lake
Cliff ●

Eagle Creek
Cliff ●

× Maggies
Peak
Elev. 8499'

Eagle Lake Cliff

Approach time: **30 minutes**

Sun exposure: **afternoon**

Height of routes: **50–110'**

Eagle Lake Cliff hosts Tahoe's highest concentration of 5.10 crack climbs all in a Wilderness area only 30 minutes from the road. On this 300-foot-wide cliff there are more than 30 routes in the 5.9-5.11 range that are 80-110 feet long, vertical, and of excellent quality. The rock is clean, fine-grained granite with few face holds. The crag rests above a picturesque alpine lake flanked by granite-covered hillsides and two 9,000-foot peaks.

At over 7,000 feet and shaded until 2 p.m., Eagle Lake Cliff offers ideal climbing on summer mornings or spring and fall afternoons. In the summer most of the climbs cook in the sun after 2 p.m. To escape the afternoon heat, climb the Eagle Head Arête, Off the Wall, or many of the routes between Changeling and Learn to Fly. If you are still too hot, adventurous climbers/cavers can explore The Chasm located behind the cliff. It features the earth's natural air-conditioning.

Toproping Beta

Half the climbs are easy to toprope by walking to the top, leaning over the edge and clipping a two-bolt anchor. For some anchors you may want a belay to get down to. A 60m rope is mandatory for toproping many climbs and a few of them require a 70m rope.

There are three options for getting to the top of the cliff and setting topropes:

1) Climb a route to the top of the cliff (the easiest ones are The Perch, Right, and Changeling).

2) Scramble to the top up the 5th class gully at the left (east) side of the cliff to the left of The Perch, Left.

3) Walk to the far west end of the cliff, walk another 50 feet, and then scramble up to the top and back east.

Chris McNamara

Approach

From "The Y" at the west end of South Lake Tahoe, drive about 9 miles (20 minutes) south on Highway 89/Emerald Bay Road and park at the Eagle Lakes Trailhead. The approach is about a mile long, takes 30 minutes, and gains 480 feet in elevation.

From the parking area, follow the trail to Eagle Lake and continue along the southeast shore to the cliff rising above the southwest end of the lake.

Descent

About half the climbs have lower-off anchors and half do not. For those climbs without lower-off anchors, there are two walk-off options:

1) The fastest descent option for climbs left (east) of Space Walk is to walk down the 4th and easy 5th class gully east of The Perch.

2) The fastest descent option for climbs west of Space Walk is to walk up away from the cliff edge for 50 feet then traverse west a few hundred feet and downclimb some 3rd and 4th class to a trail.

EAGLE'S HEAD (NOT SHOWN ON TOPO)

This pinnacle grabs your attention when you arrive at the cliff, especially in the morning light when the wild lichen and roof on the east face light up. Approach by walking up the right (west) side of the pinnacle.

Wild at Heart (not shown)   5.12b/c★★

FA: Todd Worsfold, Mike Carville, 1990.

The first route you see when approaching, with bolts visible along the insane-looking roof and arête. Can toprope with long slings from two-bolt cold shut anchor.

Rack: draws

The Criterion (not shown)   5.11a★★★

FA: Jay Smith, Paul Obanheim, J. Mitchel, 1981.

Thin crack in middle of north face. Climb past fixed pins right of roof. Two-bolt cold shut anchor.

Eagle Head Arête (not shown)   5.8★★

FA: Chris McNamara, 7/03.

Steep but bomber hand jams in a great position. Start in the corridor on the North side of pinnacle and climb up the southeast arête. Shaded most of the day. Bring long slings to set up toprope anchor of natural gear or cold shuts above Criterion.
Rack: nuts; cams: 1 ea .6-3.5"

The Perch is a good warm-up area. Lead the right crack, then easily toprope the two cracks to the left. Reach this ledge by climbing up steep 4th class rock left of Thrust is a Must.

A. The Perch, Left   5.10d★★

FA: Chris McNamara, 7/03.

Short but sustained, pumpy, and steep jams. Set toprope by making exposed spooky traverse to bolts or rap 20 feet from anchors of The Perch, Center and The Perch, Right.

B. The Perch, Center   5.10b★★

FA: Chris McNamara, 7/03.

Steep fingers, lieback, and stemming. Usually toproped after climbing The Perch, Right. Use a 2.5" piece for a directional if toproping.

C. The Perch, Right   5.9★★★

FA: Chris McNamara, 7/03.

Steep hands turns to stemming and liebacking off flakes. Can easily walk to anchors to set toprope. Bring 4.5" piece to protect last 10 feet. Bring long slings for toproping if you don't want rope running over an edge.

D. Thrust is a Must   5.10d★★★

FA: D. Grossman, Rich Van Horn, 1980.

Two committing, tenuous lieback cruxes with tricky to place gear. Can toprope with 70m rope using fixed piton as a directional.

E. Seams to Me   5.10c★★★★★

FA: D. Grossman, Rich Van Horn, 1980.

Incredible thin liebacking and stemming.

Well-protected cruxes low and high. Can toprope with 70m rope.

F. Moonflower (aka Nagual)   5.10b★★★★

FA: Bill Todd, 1976.
FFA: Rick Cashner, Angie Morales, 1979.

Slightly serious lead because the crack is filled with flexing flakes (place extra gear). Two starts: direct start has a 5.10b lieback section, or start left on Seams to Me and make a slightly runout 5.9 step right to the crack. Originally an aid climb called Nagual Wall that Rick Cashner free climbed onsight.

G. The Beak   5.10d★★

FA: Chris McNamara, Todd Offenbacher, 7/03.

Bouldery start to surprisingly steep stemming corner and tight hand crack. The crux is passing the dangling broken tooth and keeping power through the slightly overhanging jams. Use caution when placing pro behind hollow flakes. Can set a toprope by making a sideways rappel from the tree above Seams to Me or by climbing Moonflower, then traversing right to the crack and climbing up a short stretch of 5.10a to the anchor.

H. Barney Rubble   5.10b★★

FA: A. Doehring, Mike Corbett, 1980.

Powerful bulge at the start then sustained wide cracks up high. Rarely led.

I. Quest for Glory   5.10d★★★★

FA: D. Frixbee and friends, 1983.

Crux pulling through a bulge on thin finger tips with thin feet. Easy to toprope after climbing Space Truckin'. There is a cool 5.10b variation about 10 feet up on the right that connects back with the main route before the bulge.

J. Space Truckin'   5.10a★★★★

FA: Rich Cashner, Angie Morales, 1979.

A little awkward for the first 20 feet, to bomber jams. Crux is low and in the middle. The second pitch is wide, a little scary, and rarely climbed.

A. The Perch, Left 5.10d ★★ cams: 1 ea .5-3"
B. The Perch, Center 5.10b ★ cams: 1 ea .5-2"
C. The Perch, Right 5.9 ★★★ cams: 1 ea .6-3", 1 ea 4.5" (optional)
D. Thrust is a Must 5.10d ★★★ cams: 2 ea .5-2", 1 ea 3"
E. Seams to Me 5.10c ★★★★★ cams: 2 ea .4-1.75", 1 ea 2-3.5"
F. Moonflower 5.10b ★★★★ cams: 1-2 ea .5-3"
G. The Beak 5.10d ★★★ cams: 2 ea .6-3"
H. Barney Rubble 5.10b ★

I. Quest for Glory 5.10d ★★★★ cams: 2 ea .4-1.25", 1 ea 1.5-3"
J. Space Truckin' 5.10a ★★★ cams: 2 ea .75-3.5"

K. Space Walk　　　　　5.11c★★★★★
FA: Kevin Nelson, Bill Todd, 1973.
FFA: Rich Cashner, Rick Sumner, 1979.

Some have called this "the best crack in Tahoe." With its gently overhanging gold rock and laser cut crack, it's certainly one of the most aesthetic. A little awkward in the flared left crack down low and then powerful and pumpy to the top.

L. Separated Reality　　　　　5.8★★
FA: R. Clegg, K. Volz, 1973.

Stout chimney. Rarely led. Questionable protection.

M. The Vulture　　　　　5.10a★★
FA: Jay Smith, Paul Crawford, Paul Obanheim, 1985.

Looks like a gnarly owl.

N. Off the Wall　　　　　5.10c★★★★
FA: D. Rennick, K. Volz, 1973; FFA: unknown.

Technical lieback on the arête. Almost runout so you should be a confident 5.10c leader. The second clip is scary if you're shorter than 5' 10". Easy to toprope after climbing bolted chimney. From the same anchor, consider toproping the right arête that has a few different 5.11 variations, depending how much you stay on the atête. This is a great climb in the afternoon because cool air from inside the cliff hits the belayer.

O. Unknown　　　　　5.8★★★
FA: unknown

Bolted chimney that gets wider and more difficult the higher you climb. Well-protected. After climb, don't miss toproping Off the Wall.

P. Trust is a Must　　　　　5.10d★★★
FA: Todd Offenbacher, Chris McNamara, Brad Jackson, 7/03.

Technical stemming and thin face start gives way to easier climbing on big edges. From anchor, can toprope Flight Simulator. Can set toprope by walking to top or first climbing Changeling.

Q. Flight Simulator　　　　　5.11a★★
FA: Chris McNamara, Brad Jackson, Todd Offenbacher, 7/03.

Steep and unrelenting jams for 30 feet, then step left to last three bolts of Trust is a Must.

R. Changeling　　　　　5.9★★★
FA: Paul Tear, K. Haddock, 1982.

Overhanging fingers and tight hands to lieback on arête. Can toprope with 10-foot slings from Trust is a Must anchor.

S. Buster Brown　　　　　5.10b★★★
FA: Rick Cashner, Mike Corbett, 1979.

Optional 5.10b tight hands direct start, then featured corner to the amazing headwall, where overhanging hands turn to sustained fists. Need extra long slings to set a toprope.

T. Block Buster　　　　　5.9★★
Same start as Buster Brown but a lower-angle finish.

NOTE: To set topropes for Master Race through Learn to Fly, hike west along the base of the wall until you can climb 4th and easy 5th class ledges back up and left.

U. Master Race　　　　　5.11c★★
FA: Jay Smith, Paul Crawford, Paul Obanheim, 1985.

Short but stout toprope on the left arête.

V. Der Fuhrer　　　　　5.11d★★★
FA: Jay Smith, Paul Crawford, Paul Obanheim, 1985.

Another cool and bouldery toprope problem.

W. Master of Disaster　　　　　5.10b★★★
FA: Paul Obanheim, J. Mitchell, 1985.

Great steep crack with liebacking, hand jams and fingerlocks. Easy to toprope after climbing Learn to Fly.

X. Learn to Fly　　　　　5.10a★★
FA: Todd Offenbacher, Chris McNamara, Brad Jackson, 7/03.

Good warm-up. Climb knobs on arête in front of the big tree. Bring long slings for anchor to avoid rope drag when toproping.

THE CHASM

If the afternoon heat is getting to you, then explore The Chasm, a 20-foot wide and 70-foot-deep depression/cave behind Eagle Lake Cliff. Enjoy the adventurous climbing/spelunking or just find a flat rock and lounge in the cool air. There are three established routes and at least three more to be done.

Y. Climate Control   5.6★★

FA: unknown

Start at the east end of the cliff and downclimb or start on the west end and climb up. This adventure is about 300 feet long and takes you from a point behind the top of The Perch all the way to Changeling. There are a few sections of 5.6 chimneying where you don't want to fall.

Z. North Chasm Crack   5.11c★★★★

FA: Aidan Maguire, Joel Moore, 1999.

This 60-foot crack is located behind the tree behind the Thrust is a Must anchor. Usually toproped from above by lowering into the chasm and climbing back out.

AA. South Chasm Crack   5.11d★★

FA: unknown

Similar quality, logistics, and difficulty to North Chasm Crack.

K. Space Walk 5.11c★★★★★ nuts; cams: 2 ea .5-2"
L. Separated Reality 5.8★★
M. The Vulture 5.10a★★ wide stuff
N. Off the Wall 5.10c★★★★ 4 draws
O. Unknown 5.8★★★ 8 draws
P. Trust is a Must 5.10d★★★ 7 draws
Q. Flight Simulator 5.11a★★ nuts; cams: 1 ea .6-4"
R. Changeling 5.9★★ cams: 1-2 ea .6-2"
S. Buster Brown 5.10b★★★ cams: 2 ea .75-4"

T. Block Buster 5.9★★ cams: 1-2 ea .4-4.5"
U. Master Race 5.11c★★ (toprope)
V. Der Fuhrer 5.11d★★★ (toprope)
W. Master of Disaster 5.10b★★★ cams: 1-2 ea .5-3"
X. Learn To Fly 5.10a★★★ 3 draws
Y. Climate Control 5.6★★★ cams: 1-2 ea .5-1.5" (optional)
Z. North Chasm Crack 5.11c★★★★ nuts; cams: 1-2 ea .5-2"
AA. South Chasm Crack 5.11d★★ nuts; cams: 1-2 ea .5-2"

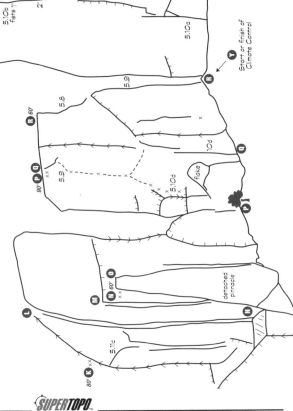

Eagle Creek Cliff

Approach time: **45 minutes**

Sun exposure: **noon to sunset**

Height of routes: **80–140'**

Eagle Creek Cliff is a larger, more broken, and slightly lower angle version of Eagle Lake Cliff. Whereas Eagle Lake Cliff has more Yosemite-style cracks, this has more featured cracks, face holds, and edges. While only a few hundred feet from Eagle Lake Cliff, it sits in a narrow canyon and remains hidden until you reach the base.

Climb on hot summer mornings when the climbs are shaded or on cold spring or fall afternoons when the routes go into the sun. If you show up and the routes are too cold, then walk across the river to the Eagle's Nest. Because the climbs are above a seasonally raging river, it's smart to bring a water filter so you don't have to carry water on the 45-minute approach.

Toprope Beta

Only the tops of routes on the left side (routes A-C) can be easily accessed to establish topropes. All the routes can be toproped after climbing a 5.10a or a 5.10b. A 60m rope lets you toprope most climbs but a 70m rope is more convenient.

Approach

Follow the approach for Eagle Lake Cliff. From below Spacewalk and the large detached pinnacle, scramble down and west over talus until you are 50 feet from the river. For routes A-C, walk parallel to the river for a few hundred feet to the left side of the cliff.

The remaining routes are on the far right (west) side of the cliff. Follow a climbers' trail that enters the brush, staying equidistant from the river and the cliff. After about a hundred yards you reach the right side of the cliff.

GPS Coordinate below Between Two Worlds: 38° 56' 409", 120° 07' 468"

Chris McNamara

Descent

Rappel all routes to descend.

A. Here and Now   5.10a★★★

FA: Chris McNamara, 9/03.

Good warm-up. Tight hands, fingers, and stemming. When toproping, most climbers avoid the last 40 dirty feet.

Rack: nuts; cams: 1-2 ea .5-2"

B. Between Two Worlds   5.10b★★★★

FA: Chris McNamara, Brad Jackson, 9/03.

Sustained thin jams with a mixture of powerful and delicate moves. Easy to toprope and well-protected on gear.

Rack: nuts; cams: 2 ea .4-2"

C. Bad Perception   5.10c★★★★

FA: Chris McNamara, Brad Jackson, 9/03.

Arching steep hand crack to nearly invisible crack and face. Some tricky gear placements. Look for the knob tie-off.

Rack: nuts; cams: 2 ea .4-2", small offset brass nuts

NOTE: A 70m rope is recommended for toproping the next three routes. It's barely possible to toprope these climbs with a 60m rope (the belayer must be under the Bumble Bee start).

D. Black Ice   5.10d★★

FA: Dan Kennedy, Chris McNamara, 10/03.

Short, cool cracks between ledges. Sustained 5.10 flared crack start then traverse left at roof. One remarkable 15-foot section up high.

Rack: nuts; cams: 2 ea .4-3"

E. Frequent Flyer   5.11b★★★

FA: Chris McNamara, Dan Kennedy, 10/03.

Sustained 5.10 flared crack start to roof, then exciting technical 5.11b crux protected by tiny cams and brass nuts. Up high the crack bends right and joins with Bumble Bee. Hard onsight.

Rack: nuts; cams: 2 ea .4-2"; 1 set brass nuts

F. Bumble Bee   5.10a★★

FA: Eric Volz, Brian Cork, 9/03.

Splitter wide hand crack, then step left to cool face crack. With 60m rope can barely toprope all the routes that share the same anchor. Left of the corner, the gold arête has some fun 5.11-5.12a toprope options.

Rack: nuts, cams: 1 ea .5-1.5", 2 ea 1.75-3.5"

G. Bird Turd   5.10b★

FA: unknown

Not a great climb but the easiest way to set topropes on two climbs to the right. Some big scary blocks.

Rack: nuts; cams: 1-2 ea .75-3.5"

H. Liquid Shadows   5.10d★★★

FA: Chris McNamara, Dan Kennedy, 9/03.

Start left on the crack, reach down to clip the first bolt, then downclimb and hand-traverse right. Powerful moves on good holds. Don't miss toproping Eye of the Eagle (need 1 ea .75-3" for directionals).

Rack: nuts; cams: 1 ea 1-2"; 4 draws

I. Eye of the Eagle   5.11c★★★★★

FA: Eric Volz, Brian Cork, Chris McNamara, 9/03.

Most striking crack line at Eagle Creek Cliff. Powerful roof to pumpy hands and tight hands in leaning corner. A 5.10c variation start to the left that climbs a huge dangling hollow flake. Fun to toprope but rarely led. Must use directionals to toprope.

Rack: nuts, cams: 2 ea .6-3"

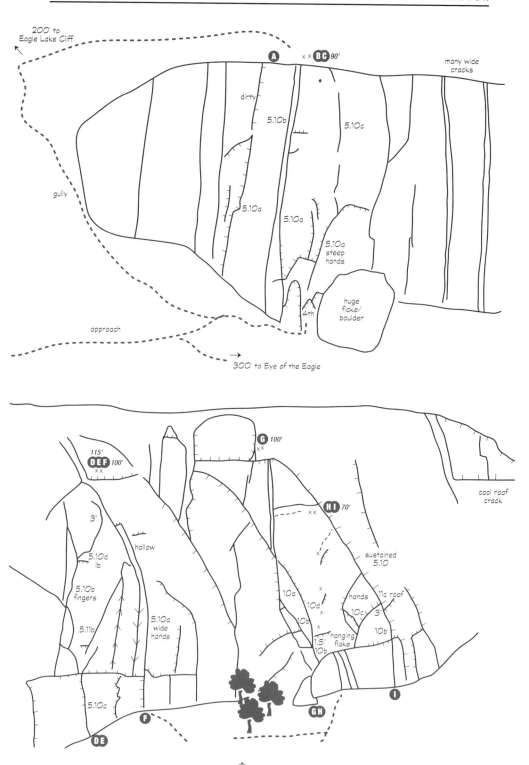

Eagle's Nest

Approach time: **40 minutes**

Sun exposure: **morning to afternoon**

Height of routes: **50–70'**

Eagle's Nest is a great training area for harder climbing and has an even more secluded feel than Eagle Lake Cliff. It's 40 to 70 feet tall and steep with tightly-spaced cracks. The rock is more featured than Eagle Lake Cliff and you often use face holds on the sides of cracks.

Eagle's Nest is usually warm in the morning and midday if Eagle Lake Cliff is too cold. Conversely, climb here to escape the sun in the late afternoon. The Hornets' Hideout cave provides shelter in a thunderstorm.

The hornet route names originated in the summer of 2003 when Eric Volz, stepped on a yellow jacket nest and was engulfed by them. He ran a few hundred yards toward Eagle Lake until, after five stings, the wasps finally relented. Meanwhile, Dan Kennedy, who was belaying near the nest, could not run. He lay down in the bushes nearby and did not move for fear the swarm would turn on him. He endured two stings.

Toprope Beta

Reach the top of the cliff to set topropes by scrambling 4th class 60 feet right of Fledgling Crack. Once the rope is on one climb, it's usually easy to move it around from anchor to anchor. A popular circuit is to start on Fledgling Crack, then climb Yellow Jacket, then Bird of Prey, then Flight School.

Approach

Follow the approach to the middle of Eagle Lake Cliff (around Spacewalk). Look across the canyon at a multi-tiered collection of gold and black broken cliffs just above the river feeding Eagle Lake. Eagle's Nest is located on the bottom tier and is the sheerest section of rock behind a big cedar tree on a ledge.

Diagonal down the talus toward Eagle's Nest. As you approach the river, locate a tunnel through the brush 200 feet east of the cliff. From the water, walk east for 20 feet down the river, then traverse back up and left (west) to the cliff.

GPS Coordinate of Eagle's Nest:
38º 56' 390", 120º 07' 538"

A. Fledgling Crack   5.10a★★

FA: Chris McNamara, Bill Cox, Dan Kennedy, 9/03.

Easiest and shortest climb on cliff, but still attention-grabbing. Good way to warm up and set topropes on other climbs. Well-protected steep jams and stemming.
Rack: nuts; cams 1 ea .5-3.5"

B. Bird of Prey   5.11a★★★

FA: Chris McNamara, 9/03.

Cool arête traverse to steep fingers on diagonally double cracks. Pumpy to place gear at crux.
Rack: nuts; cams: 2 ea .4-.75", 1 ea. 1-2.5"

C. Yellow Jacket   5.10d★★

FA: Chris McNamara, 8/03.

Stemming and squeeze moves to the thining crack.
Rack: nuts, 1-2 ea .5-1.5"

D. Flight School   5.11d★★★

FA: Chris McNamara, Kevin Swift, 9/03.

Powerful moves through roof, then steep fingerlocks, sidepulls, and face moves. Well-protected but pumpy to place gear.
Rack: nuts; cams: 2 ea .4-1.5"

E. Another WASP climb   5.12b★★★

Fun toprope off of Yellow Jacket anchor with optional directional. Climb directly above first bolt, mostly on super thin and technical face.

F. Dragon Fly   5.10b★★★

FA: Chris McNamara, Dan Kennedy, 8/03.

Steep start past bolt to hand-traverse, then steep hand and finger jamming. Well protected. Spooky to reach anchor from above. There is a powerful 5.10d direct start.
Rack: nuts; cams: 2 ea .5-3"

G. Hornets' Hideout   5.10d★★

FA: Chris McNamara, 9/03.

Poor, hard-to-protect rock at start. Cool
escape move out of a constricting chimney
to easier edge pulling.

Rack: Nuts, cams: 2 ea .5-2.5"

H. Swarm   5.12a★★

Cool, bouldery crux between easier
climbing. Good protection.

Rack: nuts; cams 2 ea .4-1.5"

Gold Mettle (not shown)   5.12a★★★★★

FA: Paul Crawford.

This climb is located on the upper of the
three tiers 200 feet west of the Eagle's Nest.
The route climbs the left crack for 20 feet
out an amazing steep gold wall, then turns
vertical.

Rack: nuts; cams: 1-2 ea .5-4"

Chris McNamara

Mayhem Cove

Approach time: **15 minutes**

Sun exposure: **morning to afternoon**

Height of routes: **300'**

Mayhem Cove is one of South Tahoe's most convenient and concentrated sport climbing areas. The climbs range in difficulty from 5.9 to 5.13 with emphasis in the 5.11 range. The rock is generally well-protected with bolts. The climbs ascend technical steep face between powerful roofs and bulges. You get a great view of Lake Tahoe and Emerald Bay. There are some trad climbs but they are not that good and therefore not included in this guide.

The lower wall is in the sun until noon and the upper wall is in the sun until about 2 p.m. In the summer, climb around Eagle Lake in the morning and here in the afternoon. The only gear you need is one 60m rope and 12 quickdraws. The bases of some climbs are dusty so bring a rope bag. Almost every climb has chain anchors.

The most popular circuit is to do the following climbs in the following order: Car Jacker, Cubic Zarconia, Diamond, and then a bunch of 5.11s on the Lower Wall.

Approach

The approach takes about 5 minutes. From just west of the bathroom in the parking area, pick up a climbers' trail that leads west. After a few feet, meet a dirt road and turn right. Walk this for a few hundred yards.

LOWER WALL

Tightly packed routes… sometimes confusing which bolts to clip.

A. Fatal Attraction   5.12a★★★

FA: Paul Crawford, Todd Worsfold, 1989.

Stout 5.12a that has a crux that doesn't end.
Rack: 4 draws

B. India Ink   5.12b★★

FA: Paul Crawford.

One-move-wonder off a powerful undercling.
Rack: 4 draws

C. The Coroner   5.12a★★

Awkward corner that wants to spit you out.
Rack: 8 draws

D. Mandatory Suicide   5.11d★★★

Powerful roofs.
Rack: 8 draws

E. Mutilated Corpse   5.11c★★★

Another cool and powerful face route.
Rack: 9 draws

F. Malice in Chains   5.11c★★★

Powerful roof, then steep sustained face. After easier broken rock, move left to anchors.
Rack: 8 draws

G. Temporary Insanity   5.11b★★★★

Incredibly sustained steep edges and underclings. Longer distance between bolts than surrounding climbs.
Rack: 6 draws

H. DWI   5.11b★★★★

Surprisingly pumpy and cool. Find the rest.
Rack: 6 draws

I. Overkill   5.11c★★★★

Start on DWI then move right into steep corner/bulge.
Rack: 8 draws

J. Car Jacker   5.9★★★

Good warm-up. Bulge low then more technical climbing up high. From anchor can traverse left and set up topropes on the many 5.11s.
Rack: 7 draws

UPPER WALL

K. Jumbolia   5.13a★★★

L. Black Rain   5.13a★★

FA: Mike Ledlinski, Tom Gilje, 1990.

M. Verbal Abuse   5.12c★★

FA: Paul Crawford, Dan Osman, 1990.

N Cajun Hell   5.13a★★★★★

This is a linkup of two routes. The first pitch, Huntin' Gator, is a very popular and fun 5.12b. The second pitch is Drinkin' White Lightning (5.12c).

Q. Gator Bait   5.13a★★★

FA: Gram Saunders, 1996.

R. Riddler   5.11a★★★★

FA: Todd Worsfold, 1990.

Many bulges on featured rock. Optional hand jams abound.
Rack: 10 draws

S. Cubic Zarconia   5.10b★★★★

FA: Dave Hatchett, Dave Griffith.

Great warm-up with alternating sections of slab and steepness. Discontinuous crack system to bulges to slab crux then final bulge.
Rack: 11 draws

T. Diamond   5.10c★★★★

Powerful crux low then a few more 5.10 sections up high.
Rack: 11 draws

Chris McNamara

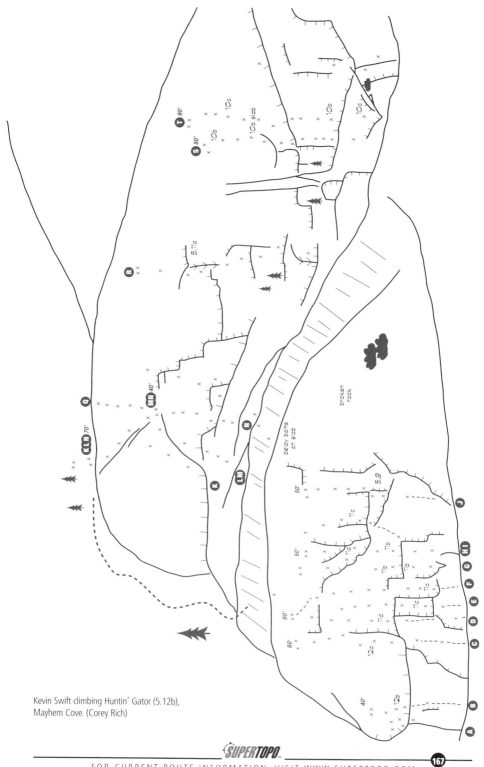

Kevin Swift climbing Huntin' Gator (5.12b),
Mayhem Cove. (Corey Rich)

90-Foot Wall

Approach time: **7 minutes**

Sun exposure: **morning**

Height of routes: **50–90'**

This is one of the most crowded and convenient cliffs in Tahoe. The climbing is fun, the approach is short, and you can easily toprope every route. The cliff offers a mixture of face and crack climbs that are polished from all the traffic.

The cliff gets sun in the morning and sun in the afternoon. To avoid crowds and summer heat, climb in the late afternoon. You can lead all climbs with a set of nuts and cams 1-2 ea .5-3". However, just about everyone who climbs here topropes.

Toproping Beta

To toprope the climbs, walk up the left side of the cliff. Most climbs have at least two bolts above them. The routes are so highly concentrated that you can usually toprope three to five climbs from a single anchor.

Approach

From the parking area, walk the Eagle Lakes Trail. After about a minute, turn right onto Eagle Loop Trail. After another few minutes, veer right up to the vista point. 90-Foot Wall is located 100 feet west of the vista point.

Chris McNamara

A. Shuman The Human 5.5
B. Rentier 5.7
C. Lost In Space 5.11a
D. Strontium 90 5.8
E. Bastille 5.11b
F. Relativity 5.10b Arête
G. Casual Observer 5.2 Chimney

H. Alias Emil Bart 5.10c
I. Ripoff 5.10
J. Never Ending Story 5.11
K. Fallout 5.9
L. Bachar's Line 5.11
M. Holdless Horror 5.6
N. Vintage 85 5.9

O. Lightning Bolt 5.10b
P. Ice Nine 5.10a
Q. Polar Circus 5.11c
R. Ti-si-ack 5.10d
S. Dave's Run 5.11b
T. One More For The Road 5.10d

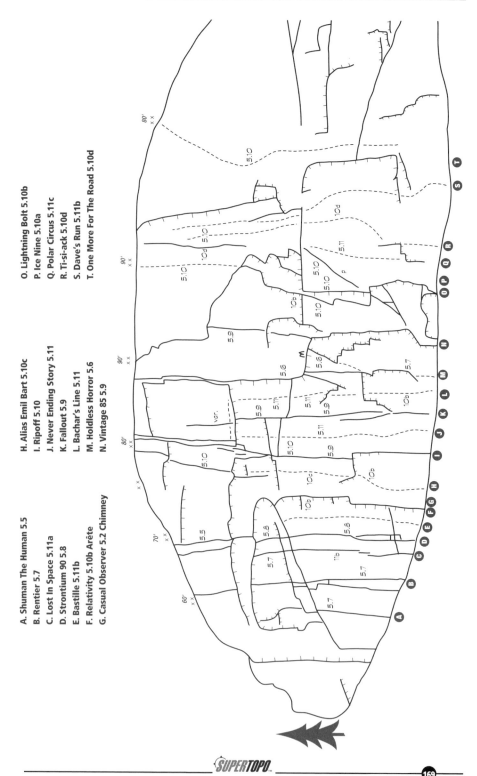

LOVER'S LEAP GUIDES
530-318-2939
www.LoversLeap.net

Climbing Instruction and Guiding for all Ages and Abilities
Self Rescue Classes
Learn to Lead Climb and Set Safe Anchors
Adaptive Climbing Classes

We need YOUR feedback

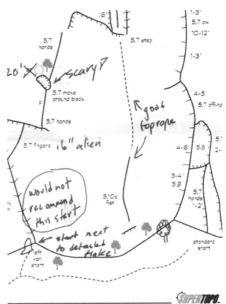

I love getting feedback on SuperTopos. The reason we make SuperTopos is so that you and other climbers can have an incredible experience on the rock. If there is any way I can make this experience better I want to know.

Every time you climb a route you will come away with a unique familiarity about each pitch. I want to hear what you thought of the climb and what you think can be improved on our topos. This information will help us make better topos and enhance other people's climbing experience.

Mail us your topo corrections and help make SuperTopos even better.

Subject: Some feedback on the SuperTopos
From: run@itout.com
To: chris@supertopo.com

The topos ruled. here is some feedback

Jam Crack ...
* Although the topo is very clear, you might want to add the words "15' left" after ".... either belay 15' left at the bolted anchor or continue ....". The reason I say that is the first time I led the climb I just kept climbing up the very thin, maybe .10d section between the top of the 5.7 crack section and the bolts. It looked really hard so I down climbed and realized I was supposed to be further left.

After Six ...
* 1st Pitch ... You might (or not) want to repeat a comment I've heard several times that the 1st pitch is the "hardest 5.6 in the valley". It's awkward after the dead tree and on the polished section in the middle of the pitch ... gravity wants to pull you out of the crack to the right. It's OK after starting the traverse to the right.
* I've always belay at the ledge in the Manzanita bushes just to the left of where the 5.6 variation 2nd pitch goes up. It's solid using the bushes

---

You will greatly help us if after your climb you do one of two things:

• Visit the web site's Climber Beta section (www.supertopo.com/route_beta) and tell SuperTopo users about the climb. What were the conditions like? Is there any extra beta? What did you think of the route?

• If you have any suggestions please email me at chris@supertopo.com or send snail mail to 2 Bradford Way, Mill Valley, CA 94941. Let me know if we got a pitch length wrong, if you disagreed with a rating, or if you think the topo could be better in any way.

Thank you for helping us improve SuperTopo,

Chris McNamara
Founder and CEO
SuperTopo

Climbs by Rating

5.1 – 5.5

- Ripoff 5.1 (168)
- Casual Observer 5.2 Chimney 5.2 (168)
- Fire Fly 5.5 R★★ (70)
- Knapsack Crack 5.5★★★ (123)
- Manic Depressive Direct 5.5★★ (124)
- Shuman The Human 5.5 (168)
- The Farce 5.5★★★ (116)
- Tyro's Test Piece 5.5★★ (62)

5.6

- Climate Control 5.6★★★ (157)
- Cuspid 5.6★★ (31)
- Deception 5.6★★★ (123)
- Harvey's Wallbangers, Center 5.6★★ (124)
- Holdless Horror 5.6 (168)
- Just Acquaintances 5.6★★ (118)
- North Ridge 5.6★★★ (58)
- Thug Lite 5.6★★★ (136)
- Unnamed 5.6★★ (64)
- Wave Rider 5.6 R★★★ (124)

5.7

- Bear's Reach 5.7★★★★★ (90)
- Cockabooty 5.7★★ (62)
- Corrugation Corner 5.7★★★★★ (104)
- Cryptogamic 5.7★★ (45)
- East Wall 5.7★★★ (92)
- Fly Trap 5.7 R★★ (28)
- Gingerbread 5.7★★★★ (56)
- Guide's Route 5.7 (147)
- Harding's Other Chimney 5.7★★ (64)
- Harvey's Wallbangers, Right 5.7★★ (124)
- Hey Y'all, Watch This 5.7★★ (147)
- Hogwild 5.7★★★★ (119)
- Jane Spy 5.7★★★★ (147)
- Lover's Chimney 5.7★★ (96)
- North Face, Pitch 1 5.7★★★ (104)
- Oedipus Rex 5.7★★★ (72)
- Over Easy 5.7★★★★ (62)
- Pop Bottle 5.7★★ (88)
- Rain Song 5.7 R★★ (63)
- Rentier 5.7 (168)
- Sacroiliac Joint 5.7★★ (45)
- Sayonara 5.7★★ (138)
- Scheister 5.7★★★★ (34)
- Slab-B 5.7★★ (148)
- Surrealistic Pillar 5.7★★★★★ (114)

5.8

- 1-bolt Arête 5.8★★★ (61)
- 2 of America's Most Wanted 5.8★★★ (136)
- Ant Crack, Left 5.8★★ (69)
- Ant Crack, Right 5.8★★ (69)
- Beer and a Hot Dog, Two Bucks 5.8★★★ (147)
- Bookmark 5.8★★★ (96)
- Brother of Plunder 5.8★★★ (109)
- Chainsaw Willie 5.8 R★★ (62)
- Cracked Tooth 5.8★★ (31)
- Deviate 5.8 R★★★★ (92)
- Dr. and The Doberman 5.8 R★★ (136)
- Eagle Head Arête 5.8★★ (154)
- East Crack 5.8★★★ (90)
- For Real Crack 5.8★★★ (114)
- Gods of Plunder 5.8★★ (109)
- Harding's Chimney 5.8★★★★ (34)
- Haystack 5.8★★★★★ (88)
- It's Better With Bacon 5.8★★★ (119)
- Ko-Ko Box 5.8★★★★ (69)
- Long Toe 5.8★★ (45)
- Lurch 5.8 R★★★ (37)
- Micro Brew 5.8★★ (88)
- Old Peculiar 5.8★★★ (138)
- Pony Express 5.8★★★★ (41)
- Preparation H 5.8★★★★ (89)
- Regular Route 5.8★★★ (63)
- See Thru 5.8★★ (147)
- Separated Reality 5.8★★ (156)
- Strontium 90 5.8 (168)
- The Chronic 5.8★★★ (136)
- The Groove 5.8★★★★ (116)
- The Left Cheek 5.8★★ (45)
- Thug Life 5.8★★★ (136)
- Unknown 5.8★★★ (156)
- Unknown 5.8 R★★ (118)
- Unnamed 5.8★ (52)
- Unnamed 5.8★★★ (68)
- Unnamed 5.8 R★★ (124)
- Up for Grabs 5.8★★★ (58)
- West Chimney 5.8★★ (40)

5.9

- ❏ Back Crack 5.9★ (148)
- ❏ Betty Ford's Route 5.9★★★★ (144)
- ❏ Blindfaith 5.9★★★ (40)
- ❏ Block Buster 5.9★★ (156)
- ❏ Blue Cab 5.9★★★ (104)
- ❏ California Love 5.9★★★★ (136)
- ❏ Car Jacker 5.9★★★ (164)
- ❏ Changeling 5.9★★★ (156)
- ❏ Corn Flakes 5.9★★★ (64)
- ❏ Deception Direct 5.9★★★ (124)
- ❏ Dog and Gri Gri, Two Bucks 5.9★★ (147)
- ❏ East Face Route 5.9★ (54)
- ❏ Fallout 5.9 (168)
- ❏ Fantasia 5.9 R★★★★★ (89)
- ❏ Farley 5.9★★★★ (36)
- ❏ Fear of Flying 5.9★★★★★ (56)
- ❏ First Stage 5.9★★★ (140)
- ❏ Gumline 5.9★★ (31)
- ❏ Hard Up 5.9★★ (62)
- ❏ Jack Corner 5.9★★★ (70)
- ❏ Jugs Revisited 5.9★★★★ (56)
- ❏ Just Jerry 5.9★★★ (147)
- ❏ Lean and Mean 5.9★★★★ (64)
- ❏ Middle Toe 5.9★★ (45)
- ❏ Mixologist 5.9★★ (118)
- ❏ Morticia 5.9★★★ (37)
- ❏ No Gaynor 5.9★★★ (119)
- ❏ Offwidth Their Heads 5.9★★ (138)
- ❏ Pickin' It 5.9★ (45)
- ❏ Psychadelic Tree 5.9★★ (94)
- ❏ Scimitar 5.9★★★★ (90)
- ❏ Scratchin' It 5.9★★ (45)
- ❏ Slowdancer 5.9★★★ (62)
- ❏ Soggy Biscuit 5.9★★ (118)
- ❏ The Diagonal, Left 5.9★★ (30)
- ❏ The Diagonal, Right 5.9★ (30)
- ❏ The Fang 5.9★★★ (34)
- ❏ The Line 5.9★★★★★ (92)
- ❏ The Perch, Right 5.9★★★ (154)
- ❏ Traveler Buttress 5.9★★★★★ (102)
- ❏ Vintage 85 5.9 (168)
- ❏ Yodeler 5.9★★★ (138)

5.10a

- ❏ 3-bolt Arête 5.10a★★★★ (61)
- ❏ Accessory Dogs 5.10a★★★★ (118)
- ❏ Anal Sex 5.9 R★★ (63)
- ❏ Arctic Breeze 5.10a★★★★ (106)

- ❏ Blue Wind 5.10a★★★ (116)
- ❏ Bumble Bee 5.10a★★ (160)
- ❏ Crispy Critters 5.10a★ (58)
- ❏ Dominion 5.10a★★★★ (37)
- ❏ Drive-by 5.10a★★★★ (136)
- ❏ Eagle Buttress, Right 5.10a★★★★ (97)
- ❏ Fat Merchant's Crack 5.10a X★★★ (40)
- ❏ Fish Supper 5.10a★★★ (76)
- ❏ Five Nine 5.10a★★★ (143)
- ❏ Fledgling Crack 5.10a★★★ (162)
- ❏ Here and Now 5.10a★★★ (160)
- ❏ Hospital Corner 5.10a★★★★★ (106)
- ❏ Ice Nine 5.10a (168)
- ❏ Jonesin' 5.10a★★★★ (144)
- ❏ Just Cause 5.10a★ (147)
- ❏ Labor of Love 5.10a★★★ (92)
- ❏ Learn to Fly 5.10a★★ (156)
- ❏ Methadone 5.10a★★★★ (144)
- ❏ Mixed Emotions 5.10a★★★★ (147)
- ❏ Penny Candy 5.10a★★★★ (65)
- ❏ Ringlock 5.10a★★★ (147)
- ❏ South Summit Bolt Ladder 5.10a★★★ (34)
- ❏ Space Truckin' 5.10a★★★★ (154)
- ❏ Stem Meister 5.10a★★★★ (104)
- ❏ Stone 5.10a R★★ (34)
- ❏ Tag Team 5.10a★★ (109)
- ❏ The Prow 5.10a★★★★★ (76)
- ❏ The Vulture 5.10a★★ (156)
- ❏ TM's Deviation 5.10a★★★★ (40)
- ❏ Unnamed 5.10a★★★ (94)
- ❏ Unnamed Toprope 5.10★ (148)
- ❏ Widow Maker 5.10a★★★ (148)

5.10b

- ❏ Avoidance 5.10b★★ (78)
- ❏ Bada-Bing! 5.10b★★★ (136)
- ❏ Barney Rubble 5.10b★★ (154)
- ❏ Between Two Worlds 5.10b★★★★ (160)
- ❏ Bird Turd 5.10b★ (160)
- ❏ Blue Note 5.10b★★ (66)
- ❏ Buster Brown 5.10b★★★ (156)
- ❏ Cubic Zarconia 5.10b★★★★ (165)
- ❏ Desperado Roof Var. 5.10b★★ (54)
- ❏ Dirty Dog 5.10b★★ (28)
- ❏ Dragon Fly 5.10b★★★★ (162)
- ❏ Fancy Dancin' 5.10b★★★ (64)
- ❏ Fingerlock 5.10b★★★★ (28)

❏ Hyperspace 5.10b★★★ (41)
❏ Jacko 5.10b★★★ (147)
❏ Knee On 5.10b★★★ (138)
❏ Knobelty 5.10b★★ (45)
❏ Lightning Bolt 5.10b (168)
❏ Magnum Force 5.10b★★★★ (106)
❏ Master of Disaster 5.10b★★★ (156)
❏ Moonflower 5.10b★★★★ (154)
❏ Peon 5.10b★★★ (138)
❏ Plane Crash 5.10b★★★ (148)
❏ Relativity 5.10b Arête 5.10b (168)
❏ Self Abuse 5.10b★★★ (30)
❏ Short Toe 5.10b★★ (45)
❏ Surrealistic Pillar Direct
   5.10b★★★★ (114)
❏ The Bowling Ball 5.10b★★★ (66)
❏ The Gamoke 5.10b★★★★ (106)
❏ The Perch, Center 5.10b★★ (154)
❏ The Prow 5.10b★★★ (62)
❏ Turning Point 5.10b★★★ (52)
❏ Undertaker 5.10b★★★ (148)
❏ Velvet Gloves 5.10b★★★★ (79)
❏ Virginia 5.10b★★★ (148)

5.10c

❏ Alias Emil Bart 5.10c (168)
❏ Bad Perception 5.10c★★★★ (160)
❏ Black Opal 5.10c★★★ (116)
❏ Blue Velvet 5.10c★★★★ (35)
❏ Bolee Gold 5.10c★★★★★ (33)
❏ Candyland 5.10c★★★★★ (64)
❏ Crushed Velvet 5.10c★★★★ (35)
❏ Daily Prayer 5.10c★★★★ (144)
❏ Diamond 5.10c★★★★ (165)
❏ End of the Line 5.10c★★★ (92)
❏ Fire Starter 5.10c★★ (148)
❏ Happy Face 5.10c★★★ (41)
❏ Hemroids in Flight 5.10c★★★ (116)
❏ Hushed Passage 5.10c★★ (109)
❏ Just Do It 5.10c★★★★ (148)
❏ Last Lock-up 5.10c★★★★ (70)
❏ Lounge Lizard 5.10c★★★★ (50)
❏ Moonshine 5.10c★★★★★ (143)
❏ Off the Wall 5.10c★★★★ (156)
❏ Salt Water Flush 5.10c★★★★ (140)
❏ Seams to Me 5.10c★★★★★ (154)
❏ Spud Crack 5.10c★★★★ (76)
❏ Tombstone Terror 5.10c★★★★★ (102)
❏ Wintergreen 5.10c★★ (28)

5.10d

❏ Black Ice 5.10d★★ (160)
❏ Burnt Offerings 5.10d★★★ (54)
❏ Candy Ass 5.10d★★★★ (64)
❏ Char Broiled 5.10d★★★★ (57)
❏ Five Tendons 5.10d★★★ (70)
❏ Gingivitis 5.10d★★ (31)
❏ Hornets' Hideout 5.10d★★ (163)
❏ Intervention 5.10d★★★ (144)
❏ Liquid Shadows 5.10d★★★ (160)
❏ Lusty Vicar 5.10d★★★ (79)
❏ Mad Dog 5.10d★★ (28)
❏ Make That Move Now Baby
   5.10d★★★★ (28)
❏ My Favorite Thing 5.10d★★★ (66)
❏ One More for the Road 5.10d (168)
❏ Plumbline 5.10d★★ (31)
❏ Quest for Glory 5.10d★★★★ (154)
❏ Robert's Crack 5.10d★★★ (56)
❏ Roofer Madness 5.10d★★★★ (96)
❏ Sciatica 5.10d★★ (45)
❏ Sinbad-Herbert 5.10d★★★★ (114)
❏ T-Bone 5.10d★★★ (56)
❏ The Beak 5.10d★★★ (154)
❏ The Fracture 5.10d★★★★★ (36)
❏ The Infinite 5.10d★★★★ (76)
❏ The Perch, Left 5.10d★★ (154)
❏ Thrust is a Must 5.10d★★★★ (154)
❏ Ti-si-ack 5.10d (168)
❏ Toothpick 5.10d★★ (31)
❏ Triple Bat Crack 5.10d★★★ (76)
❏ Trust is a Must 5.10d★★★ (156)
❏ Unnamed center route 5.10d★★★ (61)
❏ Yellow Jacket 5.10d★★ (162)

5.11a

❏ A Boy and His Arête 5.11a★★★ (112)
❏ Beer Can Direct 5.11a★★★ (112)
❏ Bird of Prey 5.11a★★★ (162)
❏ Black Pyre 5.11a★★★ (116)
❏ Boothill 5.11a★★★★ (102)
❏ Chopper Madness 5.11a★★★ (97)
❏ Expresso 5.11a★★★ (41)
❏ Flight Simulator 5.11a★★ (156)
❏ French Letter 5.11a★★ (66)
❏ Lost in Space 5.11a (168)
❏ Optischnauzer 5.11a★★★ (126)
❏ Political Shots 5.11a★ (143)
❏ Power Lust 5.11a★★★★ (104)

❏ Rehab 5.11a★★★★ (109)
❏ Riddler 5.11a★★★★ (165)
❏ Sea Slug 5.11a★★ (109)
❏ Steppin' Stone 5.11a★★★★ (54)
❏ The Criterion 5.11a★★★ (153)
❏ Unknown 5.11a★★★★ (54)
❏ Unnamed Crack/Face 5.11a★★★ (68)
❏ With Draws 5.11a★★★★ (144)

5.11b

❏ Bastille 5.11b (168)
❏ Cabin Fever5.11b/d★★★★ (58)
❏ Chip Shot 5.11b★★★ (143)
❏ Dave's Run 5.11b (168)
❏ Dr. Jeckel and Mr. Hyde
   5.11b★★★★ (72)
❏ DWI 5.11b★★★★ (164)
❏ East Corner 5.11b★★★ (88)
❏ Endless Plight 5.11b★★★★ (126)
❏ Eraser Head 5.11b★★★ (72)
❏ Frequent Flyer 5.11b★★★ (160)
❏ Gallows Pole 5.11b★★★★ (34)
❏ Hanus Anus 5.11b★★ (138)
❏ Happy Hour 5.11b★★★★ (143)
❏ Harrison Direct 5.11b★★★ (58)
❏ Leaner and Meaner 5.11b★★★ (65)
❏ Loading Dose 5.11b★★★★ (144)
❏ New Jersey Turnpike
   5.11b★★★★ (140)
❏ Sizzler 5.11b★★★★ (58)
❏ Slopey Saucers 5.11b★★★ (76)
❏ Talking Heads 5.11b★★★ (34)
❏ Taurus 5.11b★★★★★ (36)
❏ Telesis 5.11b★★★★ (36)
❏ Temporary Insanity 5.11b★★★★ (164)
❏ The Man Who Fell to Earth
   5.11b★★★ (41)
❏ Triple Decker 5.11b★★★ (79)
❏ Ultraviolet 5.11b★★★★ (78)

5.11c

❏ Anesthesia 5.11c★★★★ (106)
❏ Bar Fly 5.11c★★★★ (143)
❏ Black Magic 5.11c★★ (116(
❏ Box Envy 5.11c★★★ (126)
❏ Brother of John 5.11c★★ (109)
❏ Dog Fight 5.11c★★ (28)
❏ Drug Crazed 5.11c★★★ (108)
❏ Electra 5.11c★★★★ (72)
❏ Eye of the Eagle 5.11c★★★★ (160)

❏ Fallen Spirits 5.11c★★★★★ (144)
❏ Flight Deck 5.11c★★ (30)
❏ Freon 5.11c★★★ (138)
❏ God of Thunder 5.11c★★★★ (109)
❏ Holy Smoke 5.11c★★★★ (54)
❏ Jackass 5.11c★★★ (147)
❏ Lesbian Love 5.11c★★★★ (56)
❏ Main Line 5.11c★★★★ (106)
❏ Malice in Chains 5.11c★★★ (164)
❏ Master Race 5.11c★★ (156)
❏ Mutilated Corpse 5.11c★★★ (164)
❏ Nirvana 5.11c★★★★★ (106)
❏ North Chasm Crack
   5.11c★★★★ (157)
❏ North Face 5.11c★★ (50)
❏ Only the Young Die Brave
   5.11c★★ (41)
❏ Overkill 5.11c★★★★ (164)
❏ Polar Circus 5.11c (168)
❏ Seven and Seven 5.11c★★★★★ (143)
❏ Skism 5.11c★★ (109)
❏ Space Walk 5.11c★★★★★ (156)
❏ Spanish Flamethrower
   5.11c★★★★ (78)
❏ Stony End 5.11c★★ (108)
❏ Sugar Daddy 5.11c★★★★ (40)
❏ Sun and Steel 5.11c★★★ (138)
❏ The Fin 5.11c★★★★ (76)
❏ Unknown 5.11c★★★ (79)
❏ Yankee Dog 5.11c★★★ (104)

5.11d

❏ Bird Man 5.11d★★★★★ (34)
❏ Der Fuhrer 5.11d★★★ (156)
❏ Dewlap 5.11d★★★ (50)
❏ Essense 5.11d★★★★★ (79)
❏ Flight School 5.11d★★★★ (162)
❏ Flu 5.11d★★★★ (140)
❏ Golden Brown 5.11d★★★★ (57)
❏ Magic Box 5.11d★★★ (126)
❏ Mandatory Suicide 5.11d★★★ (164)
❏ Oil Slick 5.11d★★★★★ (76)
❏ Opus 7 5.11d★★★ (36)
❏ R.I.P 5.11d★★★★★ (102)
❏ South Chasm Crack 5.11d★★ (157)
❏ Straight Jacket 5.11d★★★ (144)
❏ The Siren 5.11d★★★ (70)
❏ Well Done 5.11d★★ (58)
❏ Whole Slot of Trouble 5.11d★★★ (52)
❏ Yards of Ale 5.11d★★★★ (143)

- ❏ Ziplock 5.11d★★★ (40)
- ❏ Bachar's Line 5.11 (168)
- ❏ Never Ending Story 5.11 (168)
- ❏ Original Route 5.11★★★★ (148)

5.12a

- ❏ 12-Gauge Shotty 5.12a★★★ (136)
- ❏ After Hours 5.12a★★★ (143)
- ❏ Beast of Burden 5.12a★★★ (34)
- ❏ Fatal Attraction 5.12a★★★ (164)
- ❏ Gold Mettle 5.12a★★★★★ (163)
- ❏ Harder Than It Used To Be
  5.12a★★★ (33)
- ❏ Hooker's Haven 5.12a★★★★ (33)
- ❏ Infrared 5.12a★★★★★ (78)
- ❏ Lelfie 5.12a★★★ (140)
- ❏ Northern Lights 5.12a★★ (41)
- ❏ Pillar of Society 5.12a★★★★ (114)
- ❏ Swarm 5.12a★★ (163)
- ❏ The Coroner 5.12a★★ (164)
- ❏ The Ghost in the Machine
  5.12a★★★★ (40)
- ❏ Unknown 5.12a★★ (52)
- ❏ Unnamed 5.12a★★★★ (72)
- ❏ Cry Uncle 5.12a R★★★ (41)

5.12b

- ❏ Acrobat 5.12b★★★★★ (78)
- ❏ Another WASP Climb
  5.12b★★★ (162)
- ❏ Dog Party 5.12b★★★★★ (126)
- ❏ India Ink 5.12b★★ (164)
- ❏ Powerbox 5.12b★★★★ (126)
- ❏ Spanish Inquisition 5.12b★★★★ (79)
- ❏ Strawbilly Tango 5.12b★★★ (112)
- ❏ The Drill Press 5.12b★★★ (138)
- ❏ The Mini Illusion 5.12b★★★★ (36)
- ❏ Witch Doctor 5.12b★★★★ (140)
- ❏ Fight the Power 5.12b/c★★★★★ (109)
- ❏ Wild at Heart 5.12b/c★★★ (153)

5.12c – 5.12d

- ❏ Captain Fingers 5.12c★★★★ (37)
- ❏ Scrubby's Crossing 5.12c★★★★★ (52)
- ❏ Silly Willy Crack 5.12c★★★★ (102)
- ❏ Stone Cold Crazy 5.12c★★★★ (108)
- ❏ Verbal Abuse 5.12c★★ (165)
- ❏ Grand Delusion 5.12d★★★★ (40)
- ❏ Voodoo 5.12d★★★★ (116)
- ❏ Unnamed left route 5.12★★ (61)
- ❏ Unnamed right route 5.12★★ (61)

5.13a – 5.13c

- ❏ Ah NUTTS 5.13a★★★★ (76)
- ❏ Black Rain 5.13a★★ (165)
- ❏ Cajun Hell 5.13a★★★★★ (165)
- ❏ Gator Bait 5.13a★★★ (165)
- ❏ Jumbolia 5.13a★★★ (165)
- ❏ Grand Illusion 5.13c★★★★★ (36)
- ❏ South Face A3★★ (50)

Eagle Lake as seen from Eagle Lake Cliff.
(Chris McNamara)

Climbs by Name

12-Gauge Shotty 5.12a★★★ (136)
1-bolt Arête 5.8★★★ (61)
2 of America's Most Wanted
    5.8★★★ (136)
3-bolt Arête 5.10a★★★★ (61)
A Boy and His Arête 5.11a★★★ (112)
Accessory Dogs 5.10a★★★★ (118)
Acrobat 5.12a★★★★★ (78)
After Hours 5.12a★★★ (143)
Ah NUTTS 5.13a★★★★ (76)
Alias Emil Bart 5.10c (168)
Anal Sex 5.9 R★★ (63)
Anesthesia 5.11c★★★★ (106)
Another WASP Climb 5.12b★★★ (162)
Ant Crack, Left 5.8★★ (69)
Ant Crack, Right 5.8★★ (69)
Arctic Breeze 5.10a★★★★ (106)
Avoidance 5.10b★★ (78)
Bachar's Line 5.11 (168)
Back Crack 5.9★ (148)
Bad Perception 5.10c★★★★ (160)
Bada-Bing! 5.10b★★★ (136)
Bar Fly 5.11c★★★★ (143)
Barney Rubble 5.10b★★ (154)
Bastille 5.11b (168)
Bear's Reach 5.7★★★★★ (90)
Beast of Burden 5.12a★★★ (34)
Beer and a Hot Dog, Two Bucks
    5.8★★★ (147)
Beer Can Direct 5.11a★★★ (112)
Betty Ford's Route 5.9★★★★ (144)
Between Two Worlds 5.10b★★★★ (160)
Bird Man 5.11d★★★★★ (34)
Bird of Prey 5.11a★★★ (162)
Bird Turd 5.10b★ (160)
Black Ice 5.10d★★ (160)
Black Magic 5.11c★★ (116)
Black Opal 5.10c★★★ (116)
Black Pyre 5.11a★★★ (116)
Black Rain 5.13a★★ (165)
Blindfaith 5.9★★★ (40)
Block Buster 5.9★★ (156)
Blue Cab 5.9★★★ (104)
Blue Note 5.10b★★ (66)
Blue Velvet 5.10c★★★★ (35)
Blue Wind 5.10a★★★ (116)
Bolee Gold 5.10c★★★★★ (33)
Bookmark 5.8★★★ (96)
Boothill 5.11a★★★★★ (102)
Box Envy 5.11c★★★ (126)
Brother of John 5.11c★★ (109)
Brother of Plunder 5.8★★★ (109)
Bumble Bee 5.10a★★ (160)
Burnt Offerings 5.10d★★★ (54)
Buster Brown 5.10b★★★ (156)
Cabin Fever 5.11b/d★★★★ (58)
Cajun Hell 5.13a★★★★ (165)
California Love 5.9★★★★ (136)
Candy Ass 5.10d★★★★ (64)
Candyland 5.10c★★★★ (64)
Captain Fingers 5.12c★★★★ (37)
Car Jacker 5.9★★★ (164)
Casual Observer 5.2 Chimney 5.2 (168)
Chainsaw Willie 5.8 R★★ (62)
Changeling 5.9★★★ (156)
Char Broiled 5.10d★★★★ (57)
Chip Shot 5.11b★★★ (143)
Chopper Madness 5.11a★★★ (97)
Climate Control 5.6★★★ (157)
Cockabooty 5.7★★ (62)
Corn Flakes 5.9★★★ (64)
Corrugation Corner 5.7★★★★★ (104)
Cracked Tooth 5.8★★ (31)
Crispy Critters 5.10a★ (58)
Crushed Velvet 5.10c★★★★ (35)
Cry Uncle 5.12a R★★★ (41)
Cryptogamic 5.7★★ (45)
Cubic Zarconia 5.10b★★★★ (165)
Cuspid 5.6★★ (31)
Daily Prayer 5.10c★★★★ (144)
Dave's Run 5.11b (168)
Deception 5.6★★★ (123)
Deception Direct 5.9★★★ (124)
Der Fuhrer 5.11d★★★ (156)
Desperado Roof Var. 5.10b★★ (54)
Deviate 5.8 R★★★★ (92)
Dewlap 5.11d★★★ (50)
Diamond 5.10c★★★★ (165)
Dirty Dog 5.10b★★ (28)
Dog and Gri Gri, Two Bucks 5.9★★ (147)
Dog Fight 5.11c★★ (28)
Dog Party 5.12b★★★★★ (126)
Dominion 5.10a★★★★ (37)

Dr. and The Doberman 5.8 R★★ (136)
Dr. Jeckel and Mr. Hyde 5.11b★★★★ (72)
Dragon Fly 5.10b★★★★ (162)
Drive-by 5.10a★★★★ (136)
Drug Crazed 5.11c★★★ (108)
DWI 5.11b★★★★ (164)
Eagle Buttress, Right 5.10a★★★★ (97)
Eagle Head Arête 5.8★★ (154)
East Corner 5.11b★★★ (88)
East Crack 5.8★★★ (90)
East Face Route 5.9★ (54)
East Wall 5.7★★★ (92)
Electra 5.11c★★★★ (72)
End of the Line 5.10c★★★ (92)
Endless Plight 5.11b★★★★ (126)
Eraser Head 5.11b★★★ (72)
Essense 5.11d★★★★★ (79)
Expresso 5.11a★★★ (41)
Eye of the Eagle 5.11c★★★★★ (160)
Fallen Spirits 5.11c★★★★★ (144)
Fallout 5.9 (168)
Fancy Dancin' 5.10b★★★ (64)
Fantasia 5.9 R★★★★★ (89)
Farley 5.9★★★★ (36)
Fat Merchant's Crack 5.10a X★★★ (40)
Fatal Attraction 5.12a★★★ (164)
Fear of Flying 5.9★★★★★ (56)
Fight the Power 5.12b/c★★★★★ (109)
Fingerlock 5.10b★★★★ (28)
Fire Fly 5.5 R★★ (70)
Fire Starter 5.10c★★ (148)
First Stage 5.9★★★ (140)
Fish Supper 5.10a★★★ (76)
Five Nine 5.10a★★★ (143)
Five Tendons 5.10d★★★ (70)
Fledgling Crack 5.10a★★★ (162)
Flight Deck 5.11c★★ (30)
Flight School 5.11d★★★★ (162)
Flight Simulator 5.11a★★ (156)
Flu 5.11d★★★★ (140)
Fly Trap 5.7 R★★ (28)
For Real Crack 5.8★★★ (114)
French Letter 5.11a★★ (66)
Freon 5.11c★★★ (138)
Frequent Flyer 5.11b★★★ (160)
Gallows Pole 5.11b★★★★ (34)
Gator Bait 5.13a★★★ (165)
Gingerbread 5.7★★★★ (56)
Gingivitis 5.10d★★ (31)
God of Thunder 5.11c★★★★ (109)

Gods of Plunder 5.8★★ (109)
Gold Mettle 5.12a★★★★★ (163)
Golden Brown 5.11d★★★★ (57)
Grand Delusion 5.12d★★★★ (40)
Grand Illusion 5.13c★★★★★ (36)
Guide's Route 5.7 (147)
Gumline 5.9★★ (31)
Hanus Anus 5.11b★★ (138)
Happy Face 5.10c★★★ (41)
Happy Hour 5.11b★★★★ (143)
Hard Up 5.9★★ (62)
Harder Than It Used To Be
   5.12a★★★ (33)
Harding's Chimney 5.8★★★★ (34)
Harding's Other Chimney 5.7★★ (64)
Harrison Direct 5.11b★★★ (58)
Harvey's Wallbangers, Center 5.6★★ (124)
Harvey's Wallbangers, Right 5.7★★ (124)
Haystack 5.8★★★★★ (88)
Hemroids in Flight 5.10c★★★ (116)
Here and Now 5.10a★★★ (160)
Hey Y'all, Watch This 5.7★ ★ (147)
Hogwild 5.7★★★★ (119)
Holdless Horror 5.6 (168)
Holy Smoke 5.11c★★★★ (54)
Hooker's Haven 5.12a★★★★ (33)
Hornets' Hideout 5.10d★★ (163)
Hospital Corner 5.10a★★★★★ (106)
Hushed Passage 5.10c★★ (109)
Hyperspace 5.10b★★★★ (41)
Ice Nine 5.10a (168)
India Ink 5.12b★★ (164)
Infrared 5.12a★★★★★ (78)
Intervention 5.10d★★★★ (144)
It's Better With Bacon 5.8★★★ (119)
Jack Corner 5.9★★★ (70)
Jackass 5.11c★★★ (147)
Jacko 5.10b★★★ (147)
Jane Spy 5.7★★★★ (147)
Jonesin' 5.10a★★★★ (144)
Jugs Revisited 5.9★★★★ (56)
Jumbolia 5.13a★★★ (165)
Just Acquaintances 5.6★★ (118)
Just Cause 5.10a★ (147)
Just Do It 5.10c★★★★ (148)
Just Jerry 5.9★★★ (147)
Knapsack Crack 5.5★★★ (123)
Knee On 5.10b★★★ (138)
Knobelty 5.10b★★ (45)
Ko-Ko Box 5.8★★★★ (69)

Labor of Love 5.10a★★★ (92)
Last Lock-up 5.10c★★★★ (70)
Lean and Mean 5.9★★★★ (64)
Leaner and Meaner 5.11b★★★ (65)
Learn to Fly 5.10a★★ (156)
Lelfie 5.12a★★★ (140)
Lesbian Love 5.11c★★★★ (56)
Lightning Bolt 5.10b (168)
Liquid Shadows 5.10d★★★ (160)
Loading Dose 5.11b★★★★ (144)
Long Toe 5.8★★ (45)
Lost in Space 5.11a (168)
Lounge Lizard 5.10c★★★★ (50)
Lover's Chimney 5.7★★ (96)
Lurch 5.8 R★★★ (37)
Lusty Vicar 5.10d★★★ (79)
Mad Dog 5.10d★★ (28)
Magic Box 5.11d★★★ (126)
Magnum Force 5.10b★★★★ (106)
Main Line 5.11c★★★★ (106)
Make That Move Now Baby
   5.10d★★★★ (28)
Malice in Chains 5.11c★★★ (164)
Mandatory Suicide 5.11d★★★ (164)
Manic Depressive Direct 5.5★★ (124)
Master of Disaster 5.10b★★★ (156)
Master Race 5.11c★★ (156)
Methadone 5.10a★★★★ (144)
Micro Brew 5.8★★ (88)
Middle Toe 5.9★★ (45)
Mixed Emotions 5.10a★★★★ (147)
Mixologist 5.9★★ (118)
Moonflower 5.10b★★★★ (154)
Moonshine 5.10c★★★★★ (143)
Morticia 5.9★★★ (37)
Mutilated Corpse 5.11c★★★ (164)
My Favorite Thing 5.10d★★★ (66)
Never Ending Story 5.11 (168)
New Jersey Turnpike 5.11b★★★★ (140)
Nirvana 5.11c★★★★★ (106)
No Gaynor 5.9★★★ (119)
North Chasm Crack 5.11c★★★★ (157)
North Face 5.11c★★ (50)
North Face, Pitch 1 5.7★★★ (104)
North Ridge 5.6★★★ (58)
Northern Lights 5.12a★★ (41)
Oedipus Rex 5.7★★★ (72)
Off the Wall 5.10c★★★★ (156)
Offwidth Their Heads 5.9★★ (138)
Oil Slick 5.11d★★★★★ (76)
Old Peculiar 5.8★★★ (138)

One More for the Road 5.10d (168)
Only the Young Die Brave 5.11c★★ (41)
Optischnauzer 5.11a★★★ (126)
Opus 7 5.11d★★★ (36)
Original Route 5.11★★★★ (148)
Over Easy 5.7★★★★ (62)
Overkill 5.11c★★★★ (164)
Penny Candy 5.10a★★★★ (65)
Peon 5.10b★★★ (138)
Pickin' It 5.9★ (45)
Pillar of Society 5.12a★★★★ (114)
Plane Crash 5.10b★★★ (148)
Plumbline 5.10d★★ (31)
Polar Circus 5.11c (168)
Political Shots 5.11a★ (143)
Pony Express 5.8★★★★ (41)
Pop Bottle 5.7★★ (88)
Power Lust 5.11a★★★★ (104)
Powerbox 5.12b★★★★ (126)
Preparation H 5.8★★★★ (89)
Psychadelic Tree 5.9★★ (94)
Quest for Glory 5.10d★★★★ (154)
R.I.P 5.11d★★★★★ (102)
Rain Song 5.7 R★★ (63)
Regular Route 5.8★★★ (63)
Rehab 5.11a★★★★ (109)
Relativity 5.10b Arête 5.10b (168)
Rentier 5.7 (168)
Riddler 5.11a★★★★ (165)
Ripoff 5.10 (168)
Ringlock 5.10a★★★ (147)
Robert's Crack 5.10d★★★ (56)
Roofer Madness 5.10d★★★★ (96)
Sacroiliac Joint 5.7★★ (45)
Salt Water Flush 5.10c★★★★ (140)
Sayonara 5.7★★ (138)
Scheister 5.7★★★★ (34)
Sciatica 5.10d★★ (45)
Scimitar 5.9★★★★ (90)
Scratchin' It 5.9★ (45)
Scrubby's Crossing 5.12c★★★★★ (52)
Sea Slug 5.11a★★ (109)
Seams to Me 5.10c★★★★★ (154)
See Thru 5.8★★ (147)
Self Abuse 5.10b★★★ (30)
Separated Reality 5.8★★ (156)
Seven and Seven 5.11c★★★★★ (143)
Short Toe 5.10b★★ (45)
Shuman The Human 5.5 (168)
Silly Willy Crack 5.12c★★★★ (102)

Sinbad-Herbert 5.10d★★★★ (114)
Sizzler 5.11b★★★★ (58)
Skism 5.11c★★ (109)
Slab-B 5.7★★ (148)
Slopey Saucers 5.11b★★★ (76)
Slowdancer 5.9★★★ (62)
Soggy Biscuit 5.9★★ (118)
South Chasm Crack 5.11d★★ (157)
South Face A3★★ (50)
South Summit Bolt Ladder
    5.10a★★★ (34)
Space Truckin' 5.10a★★★★ (154)
Space Walk 5.11c★★★★★ (156)
Spanish Flamethrower 5.11c★★★★ (78)
Spanish Inquisition 5.12b★★★★ (79)
Spud Crack 5.10c★★★★ (76)
Stem Meister 5.10a★★★★ (104)
Steppin' Stone 5.11a★★★★ (54)
Stone 5.10a R★★ (34)
Stone Cold Crazy 5.12c★★★★ (108)
Stony End 5.11c★★ (108)
Straight Jacket 5.11d★★★ (144)
Strawbilly Tango 5.12b★★★ (112)
Strontium 90 5.8 (168)
Sugar Daddy 5.11c★★★★ (40)
Sun and Steel 5.11c★★★ (138)
Surrealistic Pillar 5.7★★★★★ (114)
Surrealistic Pillar Direct
    5.10b★★★★ (114)
Swarm 5.12a★★ (163)
Tag Team 5.10a★★ (109)
Talking Heads 5.11b★★★ (34)
Taurus 5.11b★★★★★ (36)
T-Bone 5.10d★★★ (56)
Telesis 5.11b★★★★ (36)
Temporary Insanity 5.11b★★★★ (164)
The Beak 5.10d★★★ (154)
The Bowling Ball 5.10b★★★ (66)
The Chronic 5.8★★★ (136)
The Coroner 5.12a★★ (164)
The Criterion 5.11a★★★ (153)
The Diagonal, Left 5.9★★ (30)
The Diagonal, Right 5.9★ (30)
The Drill Press 5.12b★★★ (138)
The Fang 5.9★★★ (34)
The Farce 5.5★★★ (116)
The Fin 5.11c★★★★ (76)
The Fracture 5.10d★★★★★ (36)
The Gamoke 5.10b★★★★ (106)
The Ghost in the Machine
    5.12a★★★★ (40)

The Groove 5.8★★★★ (116)
The Infinite 5.10d★★★★ (76)
The Left Cheek 5.8★★ (45)
The Line 5.9★★★★★ (92)
The Man Who Fell to Earth
    5.11b★★★ (41)
The Mini Illusion 5.12b★★★★ (36)
The Perch, Center 5.10b★★ (154)
The Perch, Left 5.10d★★ (154)
The Perch, Right 5.9★★★ (154)
The Prow 5.10b★★★ (62)
The Prow 5.10a★★★★★ (76)
The Siren 5.11d★★★ (70)
The Vulture 5.10a★★ (156)
Thrust is a Must 5.10d★★★★ (154)
Thug Life 5.8★★★ (136)
Thug Lite 5.6★★★ (136)
Ti-si-ack 5.10d (168)
TM's Deviation 5.10a★★★★ (40)
Tombstone Terror 5.10c★★★★★ (102)
Toothpick 5.10d★★ (31)
Traveler Buttress 5.9★★★★★ (102)
Triple Bat Crack 5.10d★★★ (76)
Triple Decker 5.11b★★★ (79)
Trust is a Must 5.10d★★★ (156)
Turning Point 5.10b★★★ (52)
Tyro's Test Piece 5.5★★ (62)
Ultraviolet 5.11b★★★★ (78)
Undertaker 5.10b★★★ (148)
Up for Grabs 5.8★★★ (58)
Velvet Gloves 5.10b★★★★ (79)
Verbal Abuse 5.12c★★ (165)
Vintage 85 5.9 (168)
Virginia 5.10b★★★ (148)
Voodoo 5.12d★★★★ (116)
Wave Rider 5.6 R★★★ (124)
Well Done 5.11d★★ (58)
West Chimney 5.8★★ (40)
Whole Slot of Trouble 5.11d★★★ (52)
Widow Maker 5.10a★★★ 148
Wild at Heart 5.12b/c★★★ (153)
Wintergreen 5.10c★★ (28)
Witch Doctor 5.12b★★★★ (140)
With Draws 5.11a★★★★ (144)
Yankee Dog 5.11c★★★ (104)
Yards of Ale 5.11d★★★★ (143)
Yellow Jacket 5.10d★★ (162)
Yodeler 5.9★★★ (138)
Ziplock 5.11d★★★ (40)

MORE FROM SUPERTOPO

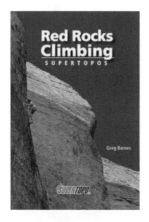

DESERT ADVENTURE CLASSICS
RED ROCKS CLIMBING (Print Book)
List Price: $24.95 Available at www.supertopo.com

Our *Red Rocks Climbing* guidebook provides SuperTopos for the best Red Rocks climbs—most in the 5.4 to 5.11 range. While the guidebook focuses on the most classic multi-pitch routes such as Crimson Chrysalis and Epinephrine, cragging routes are also included. Most of the climbs are on the highest quality sandstone Red Rocks has to offer and are well-protected with bolts or natural gear. This guide is perfect for climbers making their first trip to Red Rocks or returning climbers who want to tick off all the classics.

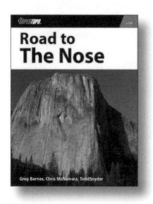

EVER WANTED TO CLIMB A BIG WALL?
ROAD TO THE NOSE (eBook)
List Price: $14.95 Available at www.supertopo.com

Many climbers consider The Nose of El Capitan the crowning achievement of a climbing career. In the *Road to The Nose*, big wall master Chris McNamara takes you through 14 climbs of increasing difficulty to help you build skills, speed, endurance, and comfort with big wall climbing. This guide includes special tips and beta specific to The Nose as well as more general information on getting ready for your first big wall.

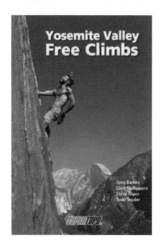

THE BEST TOPOS FOR YOSEMITE'S BEST CLIMBS
YOSEMITE VALLEY FREE CLIMBS (Print Book)
List Price: $29.95 Available at www.supertopo.com

This guidebook includes over 230 of the best routes in Yosemite Valley from 16-pitch trad climbs to one-pitch sport routes. While many hard Yosemite testpieces are included, this book focuses on topropes, crags, and multi-pitch climbs in the 5.4-5.9 range. We also include formerly obscure climbs to provide more options for avoiding crowds. As in all SuperTopo books, the authors personally climbed and documented each route with meticulous care to create the most detailed and accurate topos ever published.

MORE FROM SUPERTOPO

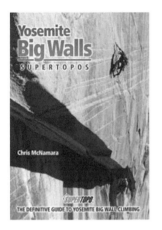

UNPRECEDENTED BIG WALL BETA
YOSEMITE BIG WALLS (Print Book)
List Price: $29.95 Available at www.supertopo.com

Written by Chris McNamara who personally climbed and painstakingly documented every route, this book includes essential route details such as climbing strategy, retreat information, descent topos, pitch lengths, and gear recommendations for each pitch. Yosemite Big Walls covers the 41 best big wall routes on El Capitan, Half Dome, Washington Column, and Leaning Tower.

OUTSTANDING PEAKS AND DOMES IN THE HIGH SIERRA
TUOLUMNE FREE CLIMBS (Print Book)
List Price: $24.95 Available at www.supertopo.com

Tuolumne Free Climbs includes over 110 of the best routes in Tuolumne Meadows from 14-pitch trad climbs to one-pitch sport routes. This book focuses on topropes, crags, and multi-pitch climbs in the 5.4-5.9 range. Includes formerly obscure climbs to provide more options for avoiding crowds. As in all SuperTopo books, the authors personally climbed and documented each climb with meticulous care to create the most detailed and accurate topos ever published.

ALPINE ROCK CLIMBING PARADISE
HIGH SIERRA SELECT (eBook)
List Price: $14.95 Available at www.supertopo.com

Included here are 14 classic High Sierra rock climbs ranging in difficulty from 3rd class to 5.10b. Most of these are well-protected, 10 to 15 pitches long, and ascend some of the best alpine granite anywhere. Whether you plan to scramble up the 3rd class East Ridge of Mt. Russell, climb the 5.7 East Face of Mt. Whitney, or ascend the epic 18-pitch Sun Ribbon Arête, this guidebook will ensure you spend minimum time getting off route and maximum time enjoying the climbing.

The Final Pitch

Chris McNamara

Thanks for buying this SuperTopo guidebook. We hope you enjoy it and the climbing adventure it may help you experience.

Your purchase means a lot to us. We here at SuperTopo are climbers who have set out to create a small business dedicated to giving you, and climbers like you, immediate access to the kind of detailed information you can normally only get by talking with a local expert. It takes a lot of work to create each SuperTopo and we're committed to making sure it's done right.

We're on a mission to develop SuperTopos for the best routes in the best climbing areas in North America. We hold ourselves strictly accountable to a high standard, namely that each of our SuperTopos offers the very finest quality route information obtainable anywhere on each and every route we cover.

If you found this SuperTopo guidebook useful, we'd like to ask you to tell your friends about SuperTopo. We're about as "grassroots" an organization as you can imagine, and are entirely dependent on word-of-mouth referrals to keep producing quality SuperTopos.

On behalf of myself and the rest of the crew here at SuperTopo, I want to thank you for your support. Keep climbing and please tell a friend about SuperTopo!

Thanks again,

Chris McNamara
Founder and CEO
SuperTopo

Chris McNamara

Climbing Magazine once computed that three percent of Chris McNamara's life on earth has been spent on the face of El Capitan— an accomplishment that has left friends and family pondering Chris' sanity. He's climbed El Capitan over 50 times and holds nine big wall speed climbing records. In 1998 Chris did the first Girdle Traverse of El Capitan, an epic 75-pitch route that begs the question, "Why?" *Outside Magazine* has called Chris one of "the world's finest aid climbers." He's the winner of the 1999 Bates Award from the American Alpine Club and founder of the American Safe Climbing Association, a nonprofit group that has replaced over 3,000 dangerous anchor bolts. He also serves on the board of directors of the Access Fund.